S. Hrg. 113–621

POWERING AFRICA'S FUTURE: EXAMINING THE POWER AFRICA INITIATIVE

HEARING

BEFORE THE

SUBCOMMITTEE ON AFRICAN AFFAIRS

OF THE

COMMITTEE ON FOREIGN RELATIONS
UNITED STATES SENATE

ONE HUNDRED THIRTEENTH CONGRESS

SECOND SESSION

MARCH 27, 2014

Printed for the use of the Committee on Foreign Relations

Available via the World Wide Web: http://www.gpo.gov/fdsys/

U.S. GOVERNMENT PUBLISHING OFFICE

94–125 PDF WASHINGTON : 2015

For sale by the Superintendent of Documents, U.S. Government Publishing Office
Internet: bookstore.gpo.gov Phone: toll free (866) 512–1800; DC area (202) 512–1800
Fax: (202) 512–2104 Mail: Stop IDCC, Washington, DC 20402–0001

COMMITTEE ON FOREIGN RELATIONS

ROBERT MENENDEZ, New Jersey, *Chairman*

BARBARA BOXER, California
BENJAMIN L. CARDIN, Maryland
JEANNE SHAHEEN, New Hampshire
CHRISTOPHER A. COONS, Delaware
RICHARD J. DURBIN, Illinois
TOM UDALL, New Mexico
CHRISTOPHER MURPHY, Connecticut
TIM KAINE, Virginia
EDWARD J. MARKEY, Massachusetts

BOB CORKER, Tennessee
JAMES E. RISCH, Idaho
MARCO RUBIO, Florida
RON JOHNSON, Wisconsin
JEFF FLAKE, Arizona
JOHN McCAIN, Arizona
JOHN BARRASSO, Wyoming
RAND PAUL, Kentucky

DANIEL E. O'BRIEN, *Staff Director*
LESTER E. MUNSON III, *Republican Staff Director*

SUBCOMMITTEE ON AFRICAN AFFAIRS

CHRISTOPHER A. COONS, Delaware, *Chairman*

RICHARD J. DURBIN, Illinois
BENJAMIN L. CARDIN, Maryland
JEANNE SHAHEEN, New Hampshire
TOM UDALL, New Mexico

JEFF FLAKE, Arizona
JOHN McCAIN, Arizona
JOHN BARRASSO, Wyoming
RAND PAUL, Kentucky

CONTENTS

Page

Alemayehou, Hon. Mimi, executive vice president, Overseas Private Investment Corporation, Washington, DC 9
Prepared statement 10
Responses to questions submitted for the record by Senator Robert Menendez 60
Responses to questions submitted for the record by Senator Benjamin L. Cardin 61
Angiuoni, Rick, Africa director, Export-Import Bank of the United States, Washington, DC 14
Prepared statement 15
Responses to questions submitted for the record by the following Senators:
Christopher A. Coons 64
Benjamin L. Cardin 65
Bob Corker 65
Coons, Hon. Christopher A., U.S. Senator from Delaware, opening statement . 1
Elumelu, Tony O., chairman of Heirs Holdings, founder of the Tony Elumelu Foundation, Lagos, Nigeria 27
Prepared statement 30
Flake, Hon. Jeff, U.S. Senator from Arizona, opening statement 3
Gast, Hon. Earl, Assistant Administrator for Africa, U.S. Agency for International Development, Washington, DC 4
Prepared statement 5
Responses to questions submitted for the record by the following Senators:
Christopher A. Coons 66
Robert Menendez 69
Bob Corker 72
Benjamin L. Cardin 74
Hart, Tom, U.S. executive director, The One Campaign, Washington, DC 39
Prepared statement 41
Response to question submitted for the record by Senator Robert Menendez 58
Hinks, Paul, chief executive officer, Symbion Power, Washington, DC 45
Prepared statement 46
Response to question submitted for the record by Senator Robert Menendez 58
Renigar, Del, senior counsel for Global Government Affairs and Policy, General Electric, Washington, DC 33
Prepared statement 35
Response to question submitted for the record by Senator Robert Menendez 59

Page

Additional Material Submitted for the Record

Written Statement from Daniel W. Yohannes, chief executive officer, Millennium Challenge Corporation 52
Letter from 13 organizations to Senators Christopher A. Coons and Jeff Flake concerning the Power Africa Initiative 53
Written Statement from Shari Berenbach, president/CEO, United States African Development Foundation 54
Letter from John Coequyt, director, International Climate Programs, Sierra Club 56
Biogas White Paper submitted by Del Renigar 79

POWERING AFRICA'S FUTURE: EXAMINING THE POWER AFRICA INITIATIVE

THURSDAY, MARCH 27, 2014

U.S. SENATE,
SUBCOMMITTEE ON AFRICAN AFFAIRS,
COMMITTEE ON FOREIGN RELATIONS,
Washington, DC.

The subcommittee met, pursuant to notice, at 10:33 a.m., in room SD–419, Dirksen Senate Office Building, Hon. Christopher Coons (chairman of the subcommittee) presiding.

Present: Senators Coons, Markey, Flake, and Corker.

OPENING STATEMENT OF HON. CHRISTOPHER A. COONS, U.S. SENATOR FROM DELAWARE

Senator COONS. Good morning. I would like to call to order this hearing of the Africa Subcommittee.

Today we will consider Power Africa, an ambitious Presidential initiative designed to double access to electrical power in sub-Saharan Africa in the next 6 years by producing at least 10,000 megawatts of more efficient, cost effective, and hopefully sustainable electricity generation capacity on the continent. By 2020, this initiative aims to increase electricity access for 20 million new households and commercial entities with a robust mix of on-grid, mini-grid, and off-grid solutions; enhance energy resource management capabilities of partner countries; and increase regional cross-border trade. These are goals I strongly support and I look forward to discussing the scope, scale, sustainability, and implementation of the initiative, as well as prospects for its future.

First, I would like to recognize Senator Flake, and we will also welcome other subcommittee members. I am grateful for Senator Flake's deep interest in this critically important issue.

And I would like to welcome our first panel of witnesses: Earl Gast, Assistant Administrator for Africa at USAID; Mimi Alemayehou, Executive Vice President of OPIC, the Overseas Private Investment Corporation; Rick Angiuoni, Africa Director for the Export-Import Bank. Our second panel will include Tony Elumelu, chairman of Heirs Holdings and founder of the Tony Elumelu Foundation; Paul Hinks, CEO of Symbion Power; Del Renigar, senior counsel for Global Government Affairs for GE; and Tom Hart, U.S. executive director for The ONE Campaign. I very much look forward to all of your insights and thank you for taking the time to be with us today.

These witnesses have been selected because of their leadership implementing and supporting this initiative either on behalf of the

U.S. Government, the private sector, or global NGOs. There are also critically important perspectives on a range of related issues, especially environmental and social impacts associated with energy development, and for this reason, I would like to enter into the record statements by the Sierra Club, Oxfam, and other organizations and thank them for their commitment and engagement on this issue. I will also enter into the record statements by the U.S. African Development Foundation and the Millennium Challenge Corporation, which plays an important role in financing power projects through its country compacts that focus on infrastructure, as well as promoting regulatory and institutional reforms in the energy sector.

Last year, President Obama committed to expanding energy access across Africa with a collaborative effort across 12 different U.S. Government agencies shown in the visual. We have committed almost $8 billion of leveraged U.S. Government resources to support Power Africa over the next 5 years, including $1 billion in MCC energy-focused compacts, $1.5 billion in OPIC loans, and $5 billion in Em-Im loans, coupled with a roughly $285 million investment by USAID. These investments have been leveraged by a robust commitment by the private sector of roughly $14 billion toward large-scale energy projects. And the six Power Africa focus countries are initially identified as Kenya, Tanzania, Ghana, Liberia, Nigeria, and Ethiopia.

Power Africa can catalyze vast opportunities for the private sector and mobilize private resources to help solve the endemic problem of energy poverty across Africa. The initiative has garnered the support of several large investors, as well as multinational institutions such as the African Development Bank and World Bank, which serve as critical partners for Power Africa. By helping to shepherd through power sector deals with regionally based transaction advisors and a capable coordinator located in Nairobi, Power Africa also aims to improve the business climate in order to attract further private sector investment in the energy sector, creating new opportunities for U.S. businesses, and promoting lasting regulatory reforms.

In some ways, most importantly, Power Africa aims to address the critical humanitarian needs stemming from endemic energy poverty across the continent. Seventy percent of the population of sub-Saharan Africa does not currently have access to electricity. That number increases to 85 percent in rural areas. When compared with other regions of the world, sub-Saharan Africa has just a tiny fraction of the electrification rates of other regions.

Businesses have cited the lack of reliable energy across the continent as the most significant impediment to doing business. Thirty percent of health facilities lack electricity. Ninety million children across the continent attend school without power, and without electricity at home, toxic fumes from kerosene and other cooking fuels lead to an estimated 3 million deaths per year. That is more than HIV/AIDS and malaria combined.

I want to make sure this initiative has bipartisan support and can be sustained over the long term in order to meet Africa's critical energy needs and accelerate U.S. private sector engagement. It is important to consider areas where the initiative can be strengthened and improved, including through its expansion and sustainable and robust budgetary support. An issue to consider is whether the number of focus countries can or should at some point be increased in order to more effectively promote access to power and encourage greater energy sector reform. This hearing will also consider how to sharpen the focus of Power Africa on distributed energy, renewables, and off-grid and mini-grid solutions, as we work together to protect the environment and address energy access issues.

As we consider the future of Power Africa, it is clear Congress, in my view, has a critically important role. This committee will soon consider legislation to authorize the initiative and address these unresolved issues, and I am pleased that today's hearing will help inform our future consideration of that bill. I am encouraged by the increased tempo of the administration's engagement on power issues highlighted by Commerce Secretary Penny Pritzker's upcoming trade mission to West Africa, the convening of the U.S.-Africa Energy Ministerial in Addis this coming June, and the U.S.-Africa Heads of State Summit in Washington this August where energy will be discussed, among other issues. The United States has taken bold steps forward in creating this Power Africa Initiative, and I look forward to working closely with the administration, with my colleagues here in the Senate and in the House to fasten and to ensure a sustained, strengthened, and successful initiative for the future.

I will now turn to Senator Flake and welcome his opening statement.

OPENING STATEMENT OF HON. JEFF FLAKE, U.S. SENATOR FROM ARIZONA

Senator FLAKE. Thank you, Senator Coons. I want to thank Senator Coons for working on this issue and scheduling this hearing and for all of you who have come to testify, particularly those who have come, like Tony, from a long way away and I really appreciate it on short notice as well. We have, obviously, those who are in positions of authority from the agencies to give us an assessment of where we are and where we are going and also technical expertise from others and people in the private sector to make sure that, as Senator Coons said, as we go through the authorization process, that we are informed in our opinions.

So with the comment, 70 percent of the population without access to electricity, it is certainly needed. This is also a big commitment in terms of funds from the U.S. taxpayer, and we want to make sure that it is directed at the right place and that we are good stewards of the taxpayer resources. We also want to make sure that bureaucratic overlap and misdirected agendas and hasty agency changes that do little to achieve the goal are mitigated here and that we move forward in ways that are both efficient and necessary.

So I look forward to the hearing today and look forward to your testimony.

So thank you again.

Senator COONS. Thank you, Senator Flake.

We will now hear from Assistant Administrator Gast, followed by Executive Vice President Alemayehou, and Director Angiuoni.

STATEMENT OF HON. EARL GAST, ASSISTANT ADMINISTRATOR, FOR AFRICA, U.S. AGENCY FOR INTERNATIONAL DEVELOPMENT, WASHINGTON, DC

Mr. GAST. Mr. Chairman and Ranking Member Flake, it is, as always, my pleasure to be here before you.

Senator Coons, before I begin, I would like to take a minute to recognize your outstanding leadership as chairman of this subcommittee. This subcommittee's commitment to development in Africa has informed our work, including Power Africa, and it has advanced our goals, and for that we thank you.

Of the 1.2 billion persons in the world who have no access to electricity, half of them live in Africa. Outside of South Africa, the 47 countries of sub-Saharan Africa generate a total of 28 gigawatts of power. That is about the same amount generated in Argentina.

There is no question that improving access to energy would multiply the impact of our development aid because it is key to building health, wealth, and education. Without light, businesses cannot operate after dark. Without electricity, hospitals cannot function, and without refrigeration, food goes bad before it reaches those who need it.

Power Africa seeks to address those issues by creating partnerships with governments, investors, and donors that will bring sustained economic growth to the people of Africa and to the United States. It is our new model for development in action, leveraging partnerships to expand access to electricity and extreme poverty, promote resilient and democratic societies, and advance security and prosperity.

Power Africa's approach multiplies the impact of every dollar we spend. Less than a year after its launch, our 35 private sector partners have pledged $14 billion to Power Africa's goals, double that which we have committed, while hundreds more companies have contacted us to find out how to get involved. Some have worked in Africa before. Many are making investments for the first time because of Power Africa. So, so far, we have already helped closed deals that will generate 2,800 megawatts of electricity. So again, in less than 1 year, we have more than exceeded 25 percent of Power Africa's goal.

And we are currently planning projects that will add 5,500 megawatts more. Some of these projects offer innovative off-grid and mini-grid solutions which can often be the best means of delivering electricity to communities that are not connected to a power grid.

Because there is no one-size-fits-all solution, Power Africa pulls the expertise of 12 U.S. Government agencies in a way that allows us to tailor our efforts and apply instruments that lock in investment. MCC, for example, which has already made major investments in power in Africa, plans to invest up to $1 billion in three Power Africa countries, Ghana, Liberia, and Tanzania, to increase access and the reliability and sustainability of electricity systems.

The U.S. African Development Foundation worked with General Electric to develop a contest seeking innovative ideas to reach off-grid communities.

The State Department is leading an effort to develop a multi-pronged power pool approach throughout the continent.

And the Commerce Department is providing a range of technical expertise, including hosting a conference this week with top United States and African energy lawyers to develop a common power purchasing agreement that will help electricity come on line quickly.

We could cite numerous other examples of our coordination, but in short, the agencies that make up Power Africa are working together like they have never done before. And that includes not only carrying out a seamless, integrated strategy, but also relying on each other to identify which of our tools need to be sharpened to accelerate our progress and which of those need to be adapted to better suit our new model for development.

Thank you again for inviting me, and thank you to the subcommittee for holding this hearing.

[The prepared statement of Mr. Gast follows:]

PREPARED STATEMENT OF ASSISTANT ADMINISTRATOR EARL GAST

Chairman Coons, Ranking Member Flake, and members of the subcommittee, thank you for the opportunity to speak with you today.

U.S. assistance to Africa is commonly thought of in terms of food, schools, clinics, and agricultural support. These are the instruments of traditional development assistance that USAID and other aid organizations have been deploying for decades. Yet our work in these sectors has limitations. With his new model for development, President Obama has added new and game-changing tools to the development toolkit. One of those tools is Power Africa.

People who lack access to cleaner, more affordable energy spend significant amounts of their limited income and resources on costly and unhealthy forms of energy like indoor fires for cooking and expensive diesel to run factories. Without light, children can't study and businesses can't operate after dark. Without electricity, life-support machines and newborn incubators in hospitals don't function. Without refrigeration, food and medicine go bad before it ever reaches those who need it. Without modern cooking fuel, homes are filled with dangerous smoke and fumes. Better access to energy will multiply our investments in reaching the Millennium Development Goals by improving health, education, and household income.

Of the 1.2 billion people in the world who have no access to electricity, half live in sub-Saharan Africa. Over a year, a refrigerator uses six times more electricity than a Tanzanian citizen, and it would take an Ethiopian citizen 2 years to consume the same amount of electricity as an American does in 3 days. Of the 20 countries with the lowest electricity consumption in the world, 17 are in Africa. Sub-Saharan Africa (excluding South Africa) generates 28 gigawatts of power for more than 900 million people—about the same amount as Argentina generates for its 41 million people. And on any given day, a quarter of that energy is unavailable due to inefficient, outdated infrastructure. Rural electrification rates are well below 5 percent in many areas—the lowest in the world, significantly lower than average rates in Asia and Latin America. And even when all of the key components are there—energy resources, technology, know-how, demand—too few energy projects make it past initial planning because the investments that would bring all of these together rarely materialize.

Yet the region has tremendous untapped sources for sustainable energy generation. Africa hosts vast reserves of natural resources, from geothermal and natural gas reserves to hydro and solar power potential. Tapping into these plentiful, sustainable resources will advance efforts to mitigate the effects of climate change, promote economic development, and improve education and health care. Cleaner energy and new technologies can power Africa's growth by bringing new businesses and jobs, and improving quality of life, while jumping past old generation technologies that pollute the environment and harm public health.

Power Africa is helping to make that happen through the U.S. Government's partnerships with African governments, private investors, other donors, and developers, which will bring sustained economic growth and benefits to the people of Africa and the United States. In six initial countries—Ethiopia, Kenya, Tanzania, Ghana, Liberia, and Nigeria—the U.S. Government will work with its partners to add 10,000 MWs of new generation capacity; increase the number of electricity connections by 20 million; increase the reliability of electricity; increase the number of countries participating in regional cross-border energy trade; and enhance the resource management capabilities of selected countries, allowing them to gain greater energy security.

The amount of investment needed for sub-Saharan Africa's power sector far exceeds the resources of the U.S. Government, African governments, and other donors. For USAID, Power Africa is our new model for development in action: facilitating private sector investment to advance development outcomes. We are discovering and supporting new and innovative ways to make our traditional development interventions become more effective and sustainable in the long run. Power Africa is creating investment opportunities and opening new markets to companies—from small businesses to multinational corporations. By leveraging U.S. strengths in energy technology, private sector engagement, and policy and regulatory reform, Power Africa is galvanizing collaboration, making quick-impact interventions, and driving systemic reforms to facilitate future investment. Power Africa uses these private sector engagements to identify the most critical policy and institutional reform issues standing in the way of these specific projects. African companies have already begun to seek out American investment partners so that they, too, can access tools that Power Africa offers from 12 different U.S. Government agencies that are working closely together to implement a comprehensive strategy.

Part of that strategy will work to advance gender equality because women and men are affected differently by energy policies and strategies due to differences—particularly concerning security—in access to electricity, as well as control over energy and energy services. That's why we are studying the relationship between gender and energy and developing approaches to leverage its relationships with the private sector, host governments, NGOs, and local communities.

What we've accomplished in less than a year's time is striking. We have helped close deals that will generate 2,486 MW of electricity—25 percent of Power Africa's 10,000 MW goal—and we are in the planning stages of projects that will add 5,579 MW more. And for every dollar that the U.S. Government has committed, the private sector has committed two, over $14 billion thus far.

There is no ''one size fits all'' solution to Africa's energy challenges, so Power Africa is serving as a conduit for pooling the expertise of the U.S. Government and other donors such as the World Bank and African Development Bank to tailor solutions to address each country's and each project's unique challenges. Power Africa is using a transaction-centered approach that concentrates on closing those deals that will have the greatest impact on improving sustainable energy access. The approach provides host governments, the private sector, and donors with incentives to encourage collaboration, provide quick results, and drive systemic reforms that will facilitate future investment.

For businesses and governments, Power Africa offers a variety of support mechanisms. African governments may establish delivery units that can help to expedite transactions. For investors and developers, Power Africa brings together the financing, insurance, and technical assistance offered by the U.S. Government to help bring power and transmission projects to fruition. U.S. Government transaction advisors are stationed in each of the six Power Africa countries to identify these potential opportunities for investment and partnership, as well as obstacles that may derail a deal. They ascertain what needs to happen to keep these deals on track, while simultaneously helping to build the capacity of existing host government ministries to deliver results.

This new model for development relies on private sector participation and private capital for success. When Power Africa was launched 9 months ago, we had secured partnerships with more than 35 partners from the United States, Africa, and other regions that collectively committed over $14 billion to achieving Power Africa's objectives. Since then, hundreds more companies have contacted us for information or assistance. Some have worked in Africa for decades; many are now evaluating opportunities on the continent for the first time because of Power Africa.

To ensure both large and small power projects are successful and meet the energy needs of the population, African governments must improve their investment climate by forming laws, regulations, tariffs, market structures, and institutions, and improving indigenous capacity to plan, design, and negotiate sophisticated transactions. Given the scale and diversity of renewable and gas resources, there is growing interest in the development of regional energy corridors and regional power transmission networks that will expand opportunities for economically and environmentally sound development for larger markets. We are working, together with other donors and international finance institutions, with existing west, south, and east power pools and looking for possible generation projects that can further cross-border interconnections and commercial electricity trade.

Consequently, a major contributor to Power Africa's success is the Millennium Challenge Corporation work to engage the African energy sector in countries eligible to receive MCC funds, Ghana, Tanzania and Liberia. MCC plans to invest up to $1 billion in these three Power Africa countries through its country compacts to increase access and the reliability and sustainability of electricity systems.

One of the most significant deals that Power Africa is helping to close is the 1,000 MW Corbetti geothermal project in Ethiopia, which promises to be the first privately owned generation project in Ethiopia. With Power Africa's assistance, the Ethiopian Government has engaged accomplished legal assistance to help negotiate its power purchasing agreement with Reykjavik Geothermal, the U.S.-Icelandic company developing the project. Power Africa's transaction advisor has been deeply involved in the deal structuring and negotiations as a neutral broker, and Power Africa and its partners are working to help reduce the drilling risk through grant facilities.

The involvement of the U.S. Government through Power Africa has also helped to increase investor confidence in Corbetti, which has expanded from an initially planned 300 MW project to up to 1,000 MW today. This project is transformational. Not only is Ethiopia opening up its energy sector to private investment for the very first time, but the Government of Ethiopia also is diversifying its energy portfolio, moving beyond large dam projects and embracing other types of renewable energy. As a direct result of Corbetti, U.S. and other companies now are exploring entering the Ethiopian energy market, and it is only the beginning for power development in the Rift Valley, which has the potential to eventually produce up to 15,000 MW of clean geothermal power.

In fact, every Power Africa country offers unique natural resources that can be developed using tailored mechanisms. In Tanzania, Power Africa helped local company Kiwari develop a 10 MW hydropower project by providing a loan guarantee through USAID's Development Credit Authority, as well as by playing an active role in negotiating the financial term sheet and loan processing associated with the $17 million project. In Kenya, as part of the Lake Turkana 300 MW wind project, which just celebrated its financial close in Nairobi on Monday, Power Africa provided technical advice that gave Lake Turkana's lenders comfort that the Kenyan electrical grid could absorb the intermittent power associated with wind farms. In addition, through the Overseas Private Investment Corporation (OPIC), Power Africa is working with the African Development Bank to provide necessary financial guarantees. Power Africa is also providing new opportunities to facilitate the growth of existing African businesses. An Ethiopian-American company is now working to develop and manufacture over 2 million smart meters for Ethiopia's power utility—in part due to a loan guarantee from USAID, as well as technical assistance funding from OPIC—to produce devices that will help reduce commercial losses and improve the efficiency of Ethiopia's national electric grid.

Reaching the most inaccessible corners of Africa's rural communities and other underserved populations is a critical component of Power Africa. Decentralized off-grid and mini-grid solutions often offer the swiftest, cleanest, and most innovative solutions to energy poverty by sidestepping the need to connect to the national electricity network. Power Africa has deployed an array of activities that explicitly target small-scale, creative energy innovation.

The Off-Grid Challenge, for instance, is a partnership between the U.S. African Development Foundation and General Electric that asked for ideas—from companies or from individuals—to develop or scale-up off-grid activities that would reach communities not served by existing power grids. Six first-round winners were selected based on the sustainability, efficiency, and impact of their projects. One Off-Grid Challenge winner, Mibawa Suppliers, will expand delivery of pay-as-you-go lighting to households in rural Kenya. Another, GVE Projects Ltd., will electrify off-grid communities using metered solar and rechargeable battery systems.

However, Power Africa's off-grid solutions are not about identifying one-off projects that may not be scalable due to the lack of interest on the part of large investors. For this reason, Power Africa continues to explore opportunities to bundle together off-grid projects so that institutional investors can deploy capital into these projects at scale.

In Kenya, Power Africa recently helped launch a 10 MW biomass project with Cummins that will use mesquite wood, a highly invasive species, as feedstock for its generator. This plant is a source of both energy and income for local residents who now will sell the wood for fuel at four times the price they currently sell for charcoal. Power Africa helped facilitate the power purchasing agreement negotiations between Cummins—a U.S. company—and the Government of Kenya. Cummins is looking to expand to add up to 18 new biomass projects in Kenya and exploring opportunities in other Power Africa partner countries. Through the U.S.-Africa Clean Energy Financing Facility managed by OPIC, Power Africa also approved technical assistance funding to support 28.5 MW in a series of potential hydropower projects in Uganda.

Power Africa is also exploring cleaner technologies that are more efficient, effective, and in some cases, even easier to set up than traditional energy sources like diesel-powered generators. We have seen how these clean energy solutions can make a tremendous difference in communities. In Kenya, Power Africa's work with government counterparts helped to expedite the development of the privately owned 60 MW Kinangop Wind Park, which will use GE turbines and is now the largest privately owned wind park in sub-Saharan Africa, outside of South Africa.

Sometimes the Power Africa contribution does not merit a front page headline, but its effects can be significant. In Nigeria, USAID's team of advisors is working with the central government on its extensive privatization plan for the electricity grid. The gradual sale of these government-owned power plants will raise much needed capital for Nigeria's Government while helping reduce inefficiencies. USAID's transaction advisor for Nigeria, a highly experienced U.S. lawyer, identified one of the key constraints preventing some deals from moving forward: the lack of a government guarantee. In response, he worked with the Nigerian Government to adapt its power purchasing agreements to include an innovative "Put Call/Option Agreement" clause that helped address that concern. That clause has now been used in 12 other deals.

In fact, this week in Washington, top U.S. and African energy lawyers who have negotiated power purchasing agreements in many of the Power Africa countries are gathered at the U.S. Department of Commerce alongside experts from international financial institutions and lawyers from Power Africa governments for a workshop hosted by the Commercial Law Development Program. Their goal for this week is to emerge with annotated, standard power purchasing agreement clauses that will significantly reduce the amount of time spent on negotiating the terms of power deals. In short, this will help electricity come online more quickly.

We also know that simply creating new energy supply will not solve the issue of cost, which remains out of reach for many Africans. We are committed to working with partner governments to ensure that these projects make energy both accessible and affordable and that our partner governments improve their legal and regulatory environment to sustain investment. For example, we are supporting the Government of Tanzania in developing its roadmap for energy reform, and the Government of Kenya in integrating renewables into its national grid.

Finally, because Power Africa's work is not over once a transaction is complete, we have created an extensive monitoring and evaluation plan to ensure that we meet our goals. We also plan to release our first annual report this summer summarizing progress.

In August, USAID established Power Africa's field headquarters in Nairobi, which has greatly facilitated interactions with the private sector and eased close collaboration with our teams at the U.S. Embassy in each of the Power Africa focus countries. As countless businesses pass through Nairobi or set up headquarters there, Power Africa's team can meet face-to-face with the businesses and speak to them directly about the constraints they are confronting and identify what the U.S. Government can do to address them.

Soon, an institutional support contract will be awarded in Nairobi, which will permit us to deploy experts in a wide range of fields on a moment's notice, to work on everything from identifying gaps and solutions for facilitating new deals to helping our African partner governments develop energy master plans. USAID already has embedded an advisor at the African Development Bank in Nairobi to work with donors and partner governments in East Africa to develop a collaborative regional geothermal development plan. Power Africa's teams in Ethiopia, Ghana, Kenya, and South Africa are also in the process of developing a strategy for strengthening power trade and regional power pools across sub-Saharan Africa.

Power Africa's strong field presence is contributing to our success. Our teams know what is happening on the ground and can convey information in real time to the Washington-based agencies for the purpose of tapping into tools and solutions. On a daily basis, the U.S. Government interagency team works together to advance transactions and push reforms, and each week, the team meets to discuss the Power Africa priority transactions, policy issues, and new opportunities. This model is working.

USAID hopes to build upon our early successes to generate momentum for additional partners and investors to support electrification in Africa.

Thank you Mr. Chairman, Ranking Member Flake, and members of the subcommittee for facilitating our assistance for African development. I welcome your questions.

Senator COONS. Thank you, Administrator Gast.

I would like to welcome Senator Corker and thank him for his support of this hearing and his engagement and interest in this topic.

Ms. Alemayehou.

STATEMENT OF HON. MIMI ALEMAYEHOU, EXECUTIVE VICE PRESIDENT, OVERSEAS PRIVATE INVESTMENT CORPORATION, WASHINGTON, DC

Ms. ALEMAYEHOU. Thank you. Chairman Coons, Ranking Member Flake, and Senator Corker, and distinguished members of the committee, thank you for your invitation to testify today.

Six hundred million people in Africa live without power. Across all of sub-Saharan Africa, the entire installed capacity is less than that of Delaware.

Nine months ago, President Obama launched an initiative to double access to electricity in Africa. He drew attention to how vital increased access to power is to shared prosperity of Americans and Africans so that children could study after dark, so businesses could start up and grow, and so Africa can begin linking to the grid of the global economy. The President proposed to extend electricity access to 20 million Africans.

Africa is ready for this initiative. OPIC has financed or insured projects in sub-Saharan Africa for more than 40 years. Annual transaction value in the region is up fourfold since 2008. The agency has more than 120 projects totaling $3.9 billion across the continent, representing about 22 percent of OPIC's total portfolio, up from 6 percent just a decade ago.

Several factors have converged to make Africa the fastest growing region in OPIC's portfolio. Number one, enormous African demand and increasing investor interests. Second is the abundance of natural resources. Third is a growing middle class with disposable income. Fourth, new U.S. investors, including members of the diaspora investing and entering the market. Five is a host-country investment climate that is actually improving by the day.

To support Power Africa, as you know, OPIC has committed $1.5 billion in financing and insurance for power projects across sub-Saharan Africa. It will also deploy its four decades of experience to help achieve the President's goal in the region.

Mr. Chairman, I am proud to report that OPIC already has a pipeline of African electricity projects that if fully committed would surpass our $1.5 billion commitment. It is a diverse pipeline, including thermal, renewable, off-grid, and biomass projects in both rural and urban areas. We have recently approved several highly developed African energy projects. Let me mention a few examples.

In Togo, OPIC is helping to finance a 100-megawatt tri-fuel facility. This plant would allow Togo to become the first exporter of power in its region.

In November, we approved funding for the Boshoff Solar Park in South Africa. This transformative project will feed 60 megawatts onto the grid.

And just last week, OPIC's board of directors approved a loan to the African Finance Corporation, which will expand AFC's energy infrastructure lending portfolio in support of power projects in Nigeria and elsewhere.

We have also financed recent energy projects in Kenya, Nigeria, Ethiopia, and Tanzania.

In addition to our projects, we have joined with the State Department and USTDA in a $20 million initiative called the U.S.-Africa Clean Energy Finance Initiative, providing small but critical elements of early funding that would allow future clean energy projects in Africa to get off the ground.

Finally, to reenergize our existing clients and reach out to new partners, OPIC and USAID later this year will be hosting a conference on African energy and infrastructure to bring investors, developers, and companies together.

Mr. Chairman, I am also happy to see that Africa's need has galvanized bipartisan support, including the recent committee approval of H.R. 2548, the Electricity Africa bill. I am especially glad to see that the Senate is also thinking about how to provide OPIC with the backing and tools it needs to do the job in Africa, backing like your support for a multiyear reauthorization to reassure long-term investors, tools like additional flexibility in the choice of financial instruments we use, and support for retaining some more of our earnings each year to support even more investments in Africa and other emerging markets around the world.

OPIC has the products that can help make this happen, our well-established and proven lending insurance and support to the private equity community. We also have the experience needed, having catalyzed more than $24 billion in power projects around the world.

With this committee's assistance, OPIC will help Africa realize its electrification potential. But we cannot do it alone. We need all the tools of the U.S. Government, the multilateral institutions, the World Bank, the African Development Bank, as well as the African governments themselves.

In closing, President Obama's vision appeals to me not only as a development finance official, but as someone who was born and raised in Africa. My grandmother spent her whole life in southern Ethiopia without ever having switched on a light. During my childhood there and later in Kenya, I saw how lack of electricity affects almost every aspect of life and work. This is real to me.

Thank you, Mr. Chairman, Ranking Member Flake, and Senator Corker and members of the other committee. I and my colleagues at OPIC are deeply appreciative of the opportunity to work on this initiative and appreciate the sustained attention and leadership of this committee. Thank you.

[The prepared statement of Ms. Alemayehou follows:]

PREPARED STATEMENT OF MIMI ALEMAYEHOU

Thank you, Chairman Coons and Ranking Member Flake, for inviting OPIC to participate in this important hearing to discuss the President's Power Africa Initiative. OPICs global development mission, its private sector focus and its proven finance and risk mitigation tools are well-suited to this initiative.

About two-thirds of Africa's people—600 million in all—live without electricity. That's nearly twice the size of the U.S. population. To put that in perspective, only about 30 percent of South Asia's population lacks electricity, and only about 10 percent of those living in the Middle East, in North Africa, and in Latin America and the Caribbean lack it. So this is a particularly African problem.

Solving the problem will unlock tremendous African social and economic potential across multiple sectors.

- African hospitals and clinics will be able to offer medicines that require refrigeration, as well as advanced medical diagnostic and treatment equipment. Health care providers will be able to treat people at more times of the day and night.
- Food can be refrigerated, reducing spoilage, improving health, and strengthening the livelihoods of farmers and grocers.
- Children will be able to study after dark and families will be able to read.
- More businesses will be able to start up and grow.
- Cellphones and laptops can remain charged, and Africa can become increasingly plugged into a global grid of information and communication.

The President's Power Africa Initiative, which is already taking shape, and is backed by increasingly broad and bipartisan support in Congress, within the business and nonprofit development communities, and in Africa itself, represents an extraordinary opportunity to change all this.

As an Ethiopian-American, this work is very personal to me. My grandmother spent her whole life in southern Ethiopia and passed away a few years ago without ever having switched on an electric light. I also spent much of my early life in Africa, where I saw firsthand the obstacles faced by families and whole communities without ready access to electricity.

BACKGROUND: OPIC IN AFRICA

OPIC has been supporting projects in sub-Saharan Africa for more than 40 years, using structured finance, business loans, political risk insurance, and private equity investment funds. Annual transaction value in the region is up over fourfold since FY08. Today, the agency has more than 120 projects totaling $3.9 billion across the continent. Today, African projects represent about 25 percent of OPIC's total portfolio, up from 6 percent a decade ago. Several factors have converged to make this the fastest growing region in OPIC's portfolio:

- Enormous African demand and increasing investor interest in the continent;
- An abundance of natural resources;
- A growing middle class with disposable income;
- New U.S. investors, particularly diaspora investors, entering the market;
- Host-country investment climates that are improving by the day.

Over $1.3 billion of OPIC's sub-Saharan Africa portfolio is devoted to financial services like microfinance lending, and loans to small and medium-sized enterprises. Other investments span sectors like agriculture and food security, health care, education, housing and technology.

Recent OPIC energy projects in sub-Saharan Africa have included:

- Three combined heat and power (CHP) plants in Nigeria that have energy efficiency as high as 90 percent and carbon capture technology sufficiently advanced to trap 95 percent of CO_2 emissions;
- The expansion of a geothermal power plant in Kenya that has added 52 MW to its previously installed capacity of 48 MW;
- $250 million in financing that is helping two American companies construct a 60 MW solar power plant in South Africa, a plant that will help South Africa avoid 140,000 tons of CO_2 emissions in its first year alone.

Currently, OPIC's energy portfolio in sub-Saharan Africa totals about $1 billion, generating 500MW of power. Globally, the energy portfolio totals $4.1 billion across 46 projects. OPIC renewable resource projects in the portfolio have seen more than a fortyfold increase since 2008.

POWER AFRICA

To support the Power Africa Initiative, OPIC will commit $1.5 billion in financing and insurance to power projects across sub-Saharan Africa. It will also deploy its four decades of sub-Saharan Africa and power project experience to help achieve the President's goals in the region.

In just the 9 months since Power Africa got underway, OPIC has made major strides in participating in a framework for interagency cooperation and in committing financing to bankable, highly developmental power projects.

I am proud to report that OPIC already has a pipeline of African electricity projects that, if fully committed, would surpass our $1.5 billion commitment.

This is a testament to OPIC's expertise in power projects, growing interagency collaboration, and the sheer demand for investment support in African power from the U.S. private sector. Our pipeline includes a diverse mix of thermal, renewable, on-grid, and off-grid projects in both rural and urban centers throughout sub-Saharan Africa. Large and small, from $250 million down to $500,000, OPIC is working across sectors and regions to provide access to energy.

In Togo, which never had its own sources of power, OPIC and a U.S. company financed a 100 MW facility that can switch between three kinds of fuel: light fuel, heavy fuel, and gas when available. When the facility is online in Togo, not only will most of Togo become completely self-sufficient in power, but the country shifts from being an energy importer to an energy exporter, selling power to its neighbors, the first country in the region to do so.

Using the new U.S.-Africa Clean Energy Finance Initiative, better known as ACEF, OPIC and its interagency partners are preparing new renewable energy projects in a collaborative way. ACEF is funded primarily by $20 million of State Department funds, of which $15 million is managed by OPIC directly and $5 million by USTDA. Through ACEF, relatively small project preparation costs are identified that impede the readiness of renewable energy projects for financing—costs like surveys, preliminary engineering work, social and environmental impact assessments, and third-party consulting fees. In just over a year, OPIC has committed nearly a third of its allotted ACEF funds, which have covered a variety of projects across seven countries.

Here are two examples:

In Tanzania, ACEF is supporting Off-Grid Electric's plans to market solar power from the mobile phone distribution platforms that are flourishing across Africa. Through ACEF, OPIC is providing $200,000 for software and analytics, hardware design, and supply chain optimization to finalize the design of Off-Grid Electric's solar home systems. Customers are able to prepay for energy via mobile phone, adjusting their usage according to their specific needs. Beneficiaries are low-income, remotely located households in Tanzania, where annual electricity usage is 92 kWh/person compared to over 13,000 kWh/person in the U.S. These solar home solutions will be affordable for 80 percent of Tanzanians, as well as more reliable and less dangerous than traditional energy sources, such as kerosene and diesel generators.

In Rwanda, only 8 percent of all households have access to grid electricity. ACEF support for Gigawatt Global, a multinational power generation project developer, with $400,000 of project development funds, has accelerated the construction of an 8.5 MW grid-connected solar power plant in the Eastern province of Rwanda. This will be Rwanda's first grid-connected solar PV project, introducing a replicable renewable energy model to the country and increasing total energy output in Rwanda by 9.3 percent. The plant will be installed on land leased from a residential community home for youth who were orphaned during and after the 1994 genocide. The Gigawatt Global project shows how a small investment on the front-end of a project can be incredibly catalytic. Because of the ACEF facility and OPIC's support, Gigawatt Global was able to reach financial close in February and expects the solar installation to be online by mid-2014. For those not familiar with the renewable energy development timeline, this is exceptionally fast.

The good news is that over the next 5 years, 7 of the world's 10 fastest-growing economies are expected to be in sub-Saharan Africa. The bad news is that energy isn't keeping up. While Africa's annual economic growth is averaging 4.5 percent or better, power generation is growing at only about 1.2 percent annually.

So OPIC is also trying to address some of the obstacles that are holding back power generation growth. Since OPIC works to facilitate transactions between the private sector in the U.S. and the private sectors in emerging markets, rather than working government to government, we can often identify government policies that stand in the way of transparent and competitive electric power generation solutions. Working with our colleagues at USAID, MCC, Treasury, Commerce, and State, we have moved these open market policy measures forward. For example, we have developed a best practices guide for Power Africa host countries and private sector investors regarding key elements of power purchase agreements.

OPIC also participates in another multiagency collaboration, called the Power Africa Working Group, that has established a wide range of private sector engagement tools and host country best practices. Importantly, it simplifies access for the U.S private sector by creating a unified one-stop shop. Power Africa has united its working group in a focused and transaction-driven approach, providing more access to electricity as part of a broader poverty reduction goal.

Thanks to this ACEF collaboration, we've seen the establishment of the U.S. Government's South Africa Energy Trade Hub, which combines the tools and expertise of OPIC, alongside our colleagues from USTDA and USAID, and the U.S. State Department.

OPIC brings to the Power Africa table its background in managing large projects and its development finance knowledge. Over the past 40 years, OPIC has committed nearly $24 billion to infrastructure projects in developing countries. Bringing these projects to completion frequently has meant working on highly complicated transactions that are time-consuming and that require the structuring of complex partnerships. Protection of U. S. taxpayers is also needed: through careful risk mitigation strategies, OPIC has kept its losses, net of recoveries, below 1 percent of portfolio value. This has allowed OPIC to return money to the Treasury for 36 consecutive years, helping reduce the federal deficit. Since FY 2008, OPIC has returned more than $1 billion to the Treasury.

While development is the primary focus of OPIC's work, we also seek to level the competitive "emerging markets playing field" for U.S. investors. In doing so, we help generate both U.S. exports and U.S. jobs.

To date, OPIC has supported more than $200 billion of investment in over 4,000 projects globally, generated an estimated $76 billion in U.S. exports and supported more than 278,000 American jobs. Over three-fourths of OPIC's 2012 projects were with American small and medium-sized businesses. And every OPIC project is empirically assessed for its development impact before funds are committed.

Based on its experience in the region and the power generation sector, OPIC believes that providing affordable, reliable energy to millions of Africans is within Power Africa's reach. Thanks to the support of Congress, the U.S. private sector and the advocacy community, we and our partner agencies are aligned in our passion to solve this global challenge.

To best utilize OPIC's ability to advance these Power Africa goals, a few key authorities are crucial including:

- Providing a multiyear reauthorization. As the U.S. Government's development finance institution, OPIC partners with the private sector in loans of up to $250 million for as long as 20 years. OPIC provides political risk insurance in some of the most dangerous parts of the world. Investors who are depending on OPIC for these long time spans want some reassurance from Congress that OPIC will continue to be there with them for the long haul.
- Supporting the President's FY 2015 budget for OPIC.

I am happy to see that Africa's electricity needs have galvanized bipartisan and bicameral support, including the recent approval of legislation in the House Committee on Foreign Affairs, on a virtually unanimous vote. I'm especially glad to see that both chambers are thinking deeply about how to provide OPIC with the backing and tools it needs to do the job in Africa. Many of the above authorities just described, are included in the House legislation and I know this committee is also considering them.

Looking ahead, OPIC will continue to increase U.S. investors' ability to access Africa's growing power sector, as well as finance and insure developmental projects across the developing world. OPIC can be nimble in taking advantage of such opportunities in part because it operates on a self-sustaining basis, at no net cost to taxpayers. In closing, I will conclude with some of my own thoughts about Power Africa.

Earlier in my testimony, I referred to my grandmother's experience of a lifetime without electricity. As an Ethiopian-American, helping to ensure Power Africa's success is more than just my job, it's an obligation to my family, friends, and birthplace. I understand how lack of electricity affects almost every aspect of life and work. The rapid advances in development that come from access to power are life-changing. I still have scores of family members and friends in both of these countries. I visit Africa often, so I associate faces and names with the task of bringing power to the continent. It's not an esoteric goal for me, but one that carries memories and real-life implications.

I feel privileged to be able to contribute something back to the place that I came from, and to the culture of which I am still a part. OPIC remains committed to investing with impact and welcomes Congress' partnership and support in the coming years.

Thank you to this subcommittee and committee for your interest in and support for this crucially important initiative. I would be happy to take any questions at this time.

Senator COONS. Thank you, Executive Vice President Alemayehou, for that moving testimony.

Director Angiuoni.

STATEMENT OF RICK ANGIUONI, AFRICA DIRECTOR, EXPORT-IMPORT BANK OF THE UNITED STATES, WASHINGTON, DC

Mr. ANGIUONI. Chairman Coons and distinguished members of the committee, good morning. Thank you for inviting me to testify today. As Director of Business Development for Africa at the Export-Import Bank of the United States, I am honored to testify, alongside my colleagues from USAID and OPIC, on the importance of the Power Africa Initiative to the United States and to Africa.

Unlike our sister agencies here today, Ex-Im Bank is not an aid or development agency. We are a financing institution with the mission of supporting U.S. jobs through exports. We require a reasonable assurance of repayment as part of our mandate.

Ex-Im Bank has a deep commitment to Africa and to Power Africa.

As you know, Ex-Im Bank is the official export credit agency of the United States. Our mission is to support U.S. jobs by empowering U.S. companies, large and small, to finance their exports. In fiscal year 2013, Ex-Im Bank supported an estimated 205,000 U.S. jobs through exports. Nearly 90 percent of the transactions the bank financed were for small business. The bank does all of this at no cost to the American taxpayers. We maintain a very low default rate of around one-quarter of 1 percent, and we did all of this while generating more than $1 billion in revenue for the taxpayers in the last year alone.

Under the leadership of Chairman Hochberg, Ex-Im Bank's global business volume has grown significantly. With respect to sub-Saharan Africa, the bank has authorized over $4 billion of transactions in the last 4 years.

Throughout our 80-year history, Ex-Im Bank has a long and successful track record when it comes to supporting power initiatives and power infrastructure development across Africa. As early as 1946, Ex-Im Bank approved a transaction to support Ethiopia's post-World War II reconstruction, including electrification.

Between 1946 and 2007, we approved power transactions in 14 African countries.

In the early 1960s Ex-Im Bank helped Ghana finance the Akosombo Dam on the Volta River. Praising this project, President Kennedy wrote to the Ghanian President, Dr. Nkruma, in 1961 saying: "It is a source of satisfaction that we have been able to join with Ghana's Government in helping to make this great day possible." And the exporter that we supported in that case was Morrison-Knudsen from Idaho who also built the Hoover Dam.

More recently, Ex-Im Bank has supported power projects in Benin, Ghana, and South Africa.

As noted by my colleagues, sub-Saharan Africa has among the lowest rates of electricity access around the world.

A key factor for the power deficit has been underinvestment in this sector in the last 20 years. If we look into the future, we know that the population of Africa is projected to increase to 1.6 billion by 2030. Therefore, it is critical that investments in the power sector are planned and executed today.

While the benefits to Africa are clear, this also presents a significant export opportunity for U.S. companies and for American job growth.

Without initiatives like Power Africa that aim to mobilize capacity investments and funding from both the public and private sectors, the power deficit in Africa is likely to become exacerbated.

Ex-Im Bank Chairman Hochberg traveled with President Obama to launch the Power Africa Initiative in June 2013.

Ex-Im Bank is a key participant in the Power Africa Initiative due to our particular capacity to support U.S. exports. As an active participant, alongside our fellow agencies, Ex-Im Bank is engaged in the Power Africa Working Group. We also maintain continuous engagement with African entities, project developers, United States exporters, and financial institutions as power projects develop across the continent.

Ex-Im Bank pledged support of up to $5 billion in support of the President's goal of doubling sub-Saharan Africa's access to electricity. And our $5 billion is a signal to African countries and investors in the African power sector that they should source equipment and services from the United States.

United States exports to sub-Saharan Africa are nominal compared to U.S. global exports. In calendar year 2013, U.S. exports to the region were $24 billion, representing about 1 percent of the U.S. global exports. Many countries are aggressively supporting their exports, and our exporters face competition not only from China but from other countries in Asia, Europe, and Latin America. Power Africa can be a catalyst for more U.S. exports, and our financing is needed to support U.S. companies. In the end, exports equal U.S. jobs.

We all know that vitalizing the power sector in sub-Saharan Africa is an enormous undertaking, but we are already seeing some progress across the region. We are beginning to see an increasing number of private sector investments complementing public sector initiatives like Power Africa. New investors are also entering the market, including U.S. companies, as well as many foreign players.

Given our mission to support American job growth, we would like to see more U.S. exporters engaged with the region and particularly the power sector.

Once again, thank you for the opportunity to testify and I am open to questions you may have.

[The prepared statement of Mr. Angiuoni follows:]

PREPARED STATEMENT OF RICK ANGIUONI

Chairman Coons and distinguished members of the Committee on Foreign Relations' Subcommittee on African Affairs, thank you for inviting me to testify before you on "Powering Africa's Future: Examining the Power Africa Initiative."

As Director of Business Development for Africa at the Export-Import Bank of the United States, I am honored to testify alongside my colleagues from USAID and OPIC on the importance of the Power Africa Initiative to the United States and to Africa.

Unlike our sister agencies here today, Ex-Im Bank is not an aid or development agency. We are a financing bank with the mission of supporting U.S. jobs through exports. We require a reasonable assurance of repayment, and we are pleased that many economies in sub-Saharan Africa have matured to the point that they can utilize Ex-Im Bank's financing.

We have a deep commitment to Power Africa and my remarks today will focus on four key areas:

- Ex-Im Bank
- Overview of the African Power Sector
- Ex-Im Bank's Role within Power Africa

• U.S. exports in sub-Saharan Africa

I. EX-IM BANK

Ex-Im Bank is the official export credit agency of the United States. Our mission is to support U.S. jobs by empowering U.S. companies—large and small—to finance their exports and win deals on the international stage. By breaking down financing barriers for U.S. firms, we contribute to a stronger national economy.

In FY13, Ex-Im Bank supported an estimated 205,000 U.S. jobs through exports. Nearly 90 percent of the transactions the Bank financed were for small businesses. The Bank does all this at no cost to the American taxpayers. We maintain a default rate of around one quarter of a percent and we did all this while generating more than $1 billion for the taxpayers in the last year alone. (This default rate is different than the default rates published in the annual Budget Appendix due to differing definitions. The reported rate in the Budget Appendix reflects projected defaults over the life of the loan while the default rate report as required in Section 89 of the Bank's charter reflects actual defaults at a particular point in time.)

Under the leadership of Chairman Hochberg, Ex-Im Bank's global business volume has grown significantly in recent years, and we are proud of our work in sub-Saharan Africa. In the last 4 years, we have authorized over $4 billion in sub-Saharan Africa transactions through our loan, guarantee, and insurance programs.

Throughout our 80-year history, Ex-Im Bank has a long and successful track record when it comes to supporting power initiatives and power infrastructure development across Africa. As early as 1946, Ex-Im Bank approved a transaction to support Ethiopia's post-WWII reconstruction, including electrification.

Between 1946 and 2007, we approved power transactions in 14 African countries. (They are: Algeria, Angola, Cote d'Ivoire, Democratic Republic of Congo, Egypt, Ethiopia, Ghana, Liberia, Morocco, Nigeria, Republic of Congo, South Africa, and Togo).

In the early 1960s, Ex-Im Bank helped Ghana finance the Akosombo Dam on the Volta River. Praising the project, President Kennedy wrote to the Ghanaian President, Dr. Nkruma, in 1961, saying: "It is a source of satisfaction that we have been able to join with [Ghana's] Government in helping to make this great day possible . . ."

More recently, Ex-Im Bank has supported power projects in Benin, Ghana, and, South Africa. Across the continent, we place a particular emphasis on clean energy development.

II. OVERVIEW OF THE AFRICAN POWER SECTOR

Sub-Saharan Africa (SSA) has among the lowest rates of electricity access in the world—less than 30 percent.

In the 2013 edition of their World Energy Outlook, the International Energy Agency (IEA) noted that sub-Saharan Africa is the only region in the world where the number of people without access to electricity is expected to deteriorate by 2030.

According to the IEA, sub-Saharan Africa will require more than $300 billion in additional investment to achieve universal electricity access by 2030.

The World Bank notes that generation capacity has been largely stagnant since the 1980s, and the entire installed generation capacity of the 49 sub-Saharan countries is about 77 gigawatts (GW) for a population of 910 million.

While there are a number of factors, the most significant reason for the power generation shortfall has been underinvestment in the power sector. The population of Africa is projected to reach 1.6 billion by 2030. Therefore, it is critical that investments in power are planned and executed today. While the benefits to Africa are clear, this also presents a significant export oppmtunity for U.S. companies—and for American job growth.

Without initiatives like Power Africa that aim to mobilize capacity, investments, and funding from both the public and private sectors, the power deficit in Africa is likely to become exacerbated.

Economic growth, social development and poverty alleviation are built on the foundation of a strong infrastructure, for which electricity is a critical component.

III. EX-IM BANK'S ROLE WITHIN POWER AFRICA

Ex-Im Bank Chairman Hochberg travelled with President Obama to launch the Power Africa Initiative in June 2013.

Ex-Im Bank is a key participant in the Power Africa Initiative due to our particular capacity to support U.S. exports. As an active participant alongside our fellow agencies, Ex-Im Bank is engaged in the Power Africa Working Group. We also maintain continuous engagement with African entities, project developers, U.S. exporters, and financial institutions as power projects develop across the continent.

Ex-Im Bank pledged support of up to $5 billion in support of the President's goal of doubling sub-Saharan Africa's access to electricity. As Chairman Hochberg likes to say, our $5 billion pledge is a signal to African countries and investors in the African power sector that they should source equipment and services from United States.

IV. U.S. EXPORTS IN SUB-SAHARAN AFRICA

Sub-Saharan Africa is now home to 6 of the 10 fastest-growing economies in the world.

The region—and particularly its rising middle class—is poised to continue to grow in relevance to U.S. export interests, and Ex-Im Bank is proud of our work in the region. In the past 4 years, Ex-Im Bank has authorized more than $4 billion in financing for U.S. exports to sub-Saharan Africa, including $604 million of authorizations in FY 2013.

The Bank approved a record 188 authorizations to sub-Saharan Africa in FY 2013. This financing supported U.S. exports to 35 of 49 sub-Saharan African countries, including Cameroon, Ethiopia, Ghana, Kenya, Mozambique, Nigeria, South Africa, and Tanzania.

As a destination market, sub-Saharan Africa receives about 1 percent of U.S. exports, but the region receives a significantly higher percentage of Ex-Im's financing. As of FY 2013, almost 5 percent of Ex-Im's total exposure was concentrated in sub-Saharan Africa.

CONCLUSION

Vitalizing the power sector in sub-Saharan Africa is an enormous undertaking, but we are already seeing some progress across the region.

We are beginning to see an increasing number of private sector investments complementing public sector initiatives like Power Africa. New investors are also entering the market, including U.S. companies as well as many foreign players. Some companies are considering retooling their production facilities to source from the U.S. and create jobs here.

We are also seeing follow-on sales for U.S. business coming from projects financed in sub-Saharan Africa.

Given our mission to support American job growth, we would like to see more U.S. exporters engage with the region, and particularly the power sector.

Once again, thank you for the opportunity to testify, and I am open to questions you may have.

Senator COONS. Thank you.

I would like to begin now a round of 7-minute questions.

Director Angiuoni—if I might just start from there and I will work my way back—I am thrilled to hear your focus on creation of U.S. jobs through exports and your recognition that there is a significant opportunity here that we are not meeting yet and would be interested in your input on the importance and relevance of long-term authorization in order to attract real partners for financing and for projects, the engagement of the diaspora community, and whether or not you think Ex-Im has the staffing, the capacity, the analytical ability to deliver on this very ambitious $5 billion commitment.

Mr. ANGIUONI. Thank you.

In the first place, it is an exciting time to work on Africa. Today there are more than 20 democracies; 20 years ago, there were only 3. The private sector is vibrant, and we have economic growth.

In terms of engaging the diaspora community, for example, we will be working with PTA Bank in terms of engaging with them and the diaspora community.

In terms of authorizations, as you know, we believe we do have the required authorization. We have a very solid balance sheet of

$140 billion. And also, as you know, Ex-Im Bank in 6 months is up to authorization. So we hope for your support on that.

In terms of staff, we believe that we have a fine team at Ex-Im Bank; the Bank and my colleagues that work on structured finance have extensive sector as well as geographic expertise.

And as part of the increase in our appropriations, which we thank you for, Chairman Hochberg is undertaking a strategic review in realigning resources, and Africa is very much on the agenda.

So we believe that we do have the authorization, and with the realignment of some of the resources, we believe we have the staffing and the expertise.

Senator COONS. Thank you.

If I might, Executive Vice President Alemayehou, roughly the same questions. How important is it for there to be long-term authorization for the Power Africa Initiative in order to attract partners, given the timeline of most power projects? You referenced in your testimony the importance of outreach and engagement with the diaspora community. If you could expand on that a little bit.

And then what portion of your portfolio is renewables or distributed generation projects? That would be of interest to me.

Ms. ALEMAYEHOU. Thank you, Senator.

In terms of long-term reauthorization, it is absolutely—absolutely—necessary for an agency like OPIC, which has a unique sort of mandate to support the private sector. As you may know, a few years back in 2008, OPIC's authorization had expired and for about 6 months OPIC cannot commit to, and disburse on, any of its investments. You can imagine, since we work with the private sector, they insist on predictability and knowing that we will be around to support them in these projects. And on infrastructure projects in particular, these are very long-term projects. The loans are sort of on our books for a very long time, and usually they take many years to come to fruition. So the fact that we will be around—there is predictability—is very important to our private sector partners.

In terms of the importance of the diaspora, obviously particularly in the African context, I myself am a member of the diaspora. I never imagined my own brother would pack up and move back to Ethiopia, which he did a few years ago, because it is sort of an exciting time in Africa.

As Rick said, we are seeing a level of interest from serious institutional investors that were never there. We are seeing—obviously, you will hear in the second panel from the private sector that are testifying—GE and others who have been there 100 years or so but are expanding their footprint. But we are also starting to see actually small- and medium-sized businesses that OPIC has worked with in other regions, in Latin America, in Asia. The example I gave you with SunEdison in South Africa; SunEdison has worked with OPIC in Latin America and other regions, but that was their first investment in South Africa. So I think one of the things Power Africa has done is that.

But in terms of the diaspora itself as a population, they have, obviously, a very direct link to the continent where they come from, and they have a very long-term perspective. So they are not investing with sort of short-term gains in mind. And when things go wrong, they also do not tend to be the first to pack up and leave. So they tend to be actually really good partners for OPIC. And our investment, as you know, has grown fourfold in the last 4 years, and some of those investments have actually been made by partnering with Ghanian Americans and Nigerian Americans who are interested in investing in their country of origin because they see huge opportunities in those countries and in those markets.

Senator COONS. Thank you.

Assistant Administrator Gast, if I might, looking at the rest of the world, electrification rates are significantly higher. In the developing world, Africa lags behind by the biggest margin particularly in rural electrification where the rates are very low.

In our own development history, the Rural Electrification Administration, or REA, launched as part of the New Deal, and the use of the co-op model, which still provides power in the rural part of my State and many other States across the country, strikes me as a powerful model worth looking at.

In your own work through USAID that has made significant progress already in providing transaction advisors, promotion of energy, governance reforms, what positive experience are you seeing that might be also applied to our work to open up rural electrification in other parts of the developing world, and what, if any, use are we making of the previous experience in the United States of electric co-ops and of our rural electrification experience?

Mr. GAST. Thank you, Senator.

So for Power Africa, as you know, we have very large transactions to help with on-grid power delivery, as well as small transactions for off-grid. And as you say, the deficit of power is much larger in Africa than any other place.

So if there is a focus on getting power to rural communities outside of Africa, what Power Africa is demonstrating now is that it can be done on a commercial basis. We are seeing this in Africa, and I assume that it is happening in other parts of the world where there is a growing business, in fact, of African businessmen who are developing small, renewable, off-grid project solutions.

With regard to your question about the rural electrification commission, AID has had a partnership with NRECA, the National Rural Electrification Cooperative Agency, for a number of years. They have done fantastic work and we are cooperating with them on Power Africa.

Senator COONS. Thank you.

Senator Flake.

Senator FLAKE. Thank you for your testimony.

Mr. Gast, the six countries that are selected—how did they make the cut or the grade there? And are those six countries—is this to be the source of power or the recipient of power? There may be cases where a hydro facility in one country feeds the other. Can you just give some indication of why we are focusing on those six countries?

Mr. GAST. Sure. To answer your second question, you are absolutely right. It could be a source of power, as well as an exporter of power. And that is one of the reasons why we are looking at power pools to help with power-sharing agreements between countries and among countries. So in the case of Ethiopia, in the coming years, within the next decade, it will be a major exporter of power, not just to Djibouti and Sudan but also to Kenya and Tanzania.

With regard to your first question, how the countries were selected; those six countries together represent about 40 percent of the 600 million persons who go without power. So we looked at it from the perspective of how can we get power delivered to the most persons on the continent quickly.

Second of all, we had to look where the private sector was interested, where the deals were being developed because the private sector is a critical component to it. If the private sector is not interested in going into a country, then this model fails.

Then third, we looked at governments making commitments to improve the regulatory and enabling environment in order to attract private investment.

Senator FLAKE. Thank you.

Can I call you Mimi so I do not have to say your last name? [Laughter.]

Not to be overly familiar.

With regard to OPIC, can OPIC be effective in its mission with the current carbon cap that you operate under?

Ms. ALEMAYEHOU. Thank you, Senator Flake.

When we made the $1.5 billion commitment over 5 years for the Power Africa Initiative, we actually made that with the cap in mind because we knew the pipeline that we had already and the power sector in the continent—we know we can meet it with the cap in mind.

Having said that, with this new ambitious legislation that was introduced in the House, we definitely need some flexibility in that so that we can do additional power projects.

Senator FLAKE. Well, thank you.

I certainly would second that. I think if the goal here is to bring power, that needs to be the goal. I know that many development experts and private sector individuals and others that I have spoken to—their main concern about this Power Africa Initiative is that it might tilt toward serving one agenda at the expense of another. I mean, if the goal is to bring power to Africa, we need to be concerned about how we best effect that, and if we need to change through legislation or otherwise these caps or mandates or stipulations that you have, I hope you will let us know what we can do.

Can you give some idea as to the mix? I think it was asked by Senator Coons, and maybe I missed the answer. What is the mix right now in terms of renewables?

Ms. ALEMAYEHOU. Sure. By the way, you know the omnibus bill removed the cap, and that would allow us to do an additional 300 to 700 megawatts.

In terms of the mix, right now in our portfolio, we have about $1.7 billion in our pipeline. I would say a third of that is actually renewable and two-thirds is thermal.

Last year, overall, in terms of our portfolio, a third was in renewables, actually to your question earlier, Senator Coons. So we have actually had a pretty robust growth in terms of renewables globally, not just in Africa.

Senator FLAKE. But, Mr. Angiuoni, give us some indication of what our competitors are doing or other countries. What is China doing in this field? Your job is to make sure that U.S. exporters have options and the opportunity and ability to play in these countries. What are some of the other countries doing, particularly China?

Mr. ANGIUONI. Thank you for the question.

As you well know, Africa has been seen as a great opportunity for countries around the world. It is not only China, as I have said in my earlier testimony. It is Europe. It is Latin America and many other countries in Asia see Africa as a tremendous opportunity not only for exports but for investments and for resources.

On the export side, it is actually quite interesting. If you look at the data provided by the U.N., the amount of imports from China represent only about 30 percent. Perhaps our biggest competitor is in Europe. The EU–27 represents about 45 percent of the imports that go into Africa. Our share of those imports is only 10 percent. So as a nation, we must do better. Our exports are increasing. Exports as a percentage of GDP is increasing. Yet, compared to other countries, it is quite low.

China is obviously quite aggressive. If you look at the energy sector, if you look at Africa, north Africa is primarily gas. The central part of Africa is primarily hydro, and the southern part of Africa, Namibia, South Africa, parts of Botswana, parts of Mozambique, is primarily coal. Where China has been extremely aggressive is primarily on hydroelectric projects. It is interesting that in the 1960s, as I mentioned in my testimony, Morrison-Knudsen helped to build the Akosombo Dam, and now primarily you have Sinohydro building dams in Africa. But I see a change in this.

Number one, I see a change that I think there is a game changer in Africa. There is 450 trillion cubic feet of gas that has been discovered in Africa, and I really think that is the future.

And also I see U.S. companies much more engaged. I think U.S. companies are realizing the opportunity costs of not being in Africa. So companies like Bechtel, who also was one of the consortium firms that built the Hoover Dam, now is looking at Africa for some big projects. So I see a greater interest in Africa and that is positive for United States jobs and United States exports.

Senator FLAKE. Thank you.

Senator COONS. Senator Corker.

Senator CORKER. Well, thank you, Mr. Chairman. I want to thank you and the ranking member for having this hearing and for your continued focus on Africa and the outstanding job that you all do here.

We, all three, have a bill on the floor here in about an hour, so I am going to ask my questions and then leave. But our staff will listen. Okay?

Thank you again for doing this.

And we are excited about Power Africa. I know we want to shape that a little differently over here in the Senate.

Ms. Alemayehou, you understand, I know—Senator Flake talked a little bit about the conflicting agendas. I know that we really have kind of cut our nose off to spite our face in years past because we have had carbon caps in Africa that have kept Africans from having power, which is not the agenda we are pursuing here. And I know you understand that a big, big piece of the power generation in the future, with the appropriations bill lifting the cap, is really going to be through natural gas. You understand that. Right?

Ms. ALEMAYEHOU. Yes, Senator. I mean, Africa, as I said in my testimony—there are 600 million people in the dark, and we are going to need all sources of energy to support those people. I believe really every country is sort of unique. Ethiopia, where I was born, 90 percent of the energy actually comes from hydro, and the rest may come from geothermal. It is clean. But as Rick was saying, in Mozambique where there are huge gas finds, probably second only to Qatar, that makes sense for that country. So I agree with you in terms of the mix of sources of energy. It has to come from every source when we are thinking about such a huge problem.

Senator CORKER. Well, listen, I am going to ask just two questions and leave.

If you would speak to—I know the private sector panel is coming up, but if you could speak a little bit to some of the difficulties the private sector is having relative to financing and why what you do is so important to this initiative, I would appreciate it.

Mr. Gast, one of the concerns that I think many people have is that we are going to end up with a lot of power generation, but a lot of times—and we have all seen this in countries we have been involved in—we do one component of it. We do not really follow through and have the discipline sometimes to force the other pieces to happen. And I think there is a big concern. We all want to see this successful I think, and I am personally very excited about this effort. But I think the distribution away from power generation, the ability to actually have tariffs that cause all of this to be self-sustainable is very important. And I wonder if you would speak to that also.

And with that, I might leave and thank you so much.

Ms. ALEMAYEHOU. Maybe I will talk a little bit about some of the challenges that we see in some of these transactions and why I think OPIC is sort of glad to be as part of the Power Africa team is sort of lack of capacity really on the government level, not just in these six countries of the Power Africa, but in some of the other countries where OPIC works at and where obviously a very tiny agency—we just have one person in South Africa. We are all sort of here in Washington. And some of the work that the transaction advisors are doing by advising these governments and these ministries on the policy and regulatory reform I think is really, really important. And I think the private sector team that is probably testifying after us may weigh in on that. But I think those are the kind of reforms that are much more long-term and will have a huge impact.

I will give you an example. In Tanzania, where we were, with USAID's assistant transaction advisor, able to change the PPA terms from 15 years to 25 years, that opened up that country's attractiveness for private sector investment in the renewable industry by doing that, not just from United States investors, but

I am talking about investors from Europe and anywhere else in the world.

And in Ethiopia's case, I think Earl talked about it in his opening testimony. Their transaction advisor there—again I think this is really huge. It is for the first time ever that country is allowing the private sector to invest in their power sector. The government until now has been able to do it on its own. They obviously cannot continue to do that. But this is huge that the fact that the country allowed the private sector to come in as a result of some of the policy and reform work that we were doing. I think that is the kind of support that would have a long-term impact on U.S. investors in the long term.

Mr. GAST. Senator Corker asked about cost-reflective tariffs, which we feel is an essential ingredient to making this a successful initiative. And, in fact, the governments make commitments as well. When they sign on to Power Africa, one of the commitments that they make is that they will move to cost-reflective tariffs. And we have already seen Ghana and Tanzania increase significantly, by 40 percent, their tariffs within the last few months. So that is a good first step.

It also leads to a bankable deal. Without a cost-reflective tariff, lenders are not going to lend and investors will not invest. So that is absolutely critical.

Senator Corker also asked about while we are focusing on generation, are we looking at the big picture. And we absolutely are. And that is where our other development partners come into play, the African Development Bank, the World Bank, MCC. The transmission costs are huge, and without the investments of the multilateral development banks, these projects also will not be bankable.

So we have integrated strategies built around the country's generation plans, as well as each individual project. And so what we are trying to do is ensure that we have sequenced investments coming in in all areas of the energy sector to make these projects viable.

Senator COONS. Thank you to the panel. If we might, we have votes scheduled for noon, which is in part why Ranking Member Corker left. I want to ask one or two more questions, if I might, and then forgive me. We have a robust second panel as well.

In terms of plans, if I could, Assistant Administrator Gast, what plans are there to consider future expansion of Power Africa beyond these six focus countries? And has USAID considered a dedicated line item? You are carrying most of the operating costs of providing these transaction advisors, these in-country teams. It would be easier for appropriators to specifically support a dedicated program line.

And then last, if I might. The Foreign Commercial Service. It is reported in some settings that China has, I think, 10 commercial officers in Nairobi alone. We have fewer than that on the entire continent. To your point, Ms. Alemayehou, there are not enough U.S. agency staff on the continent to help actually facilitate and move these deals through. What additional assistance are you getting from some of the coordinate agencies like the Department of Energy, which has relevant labs and capability particularly in renewables and in grid management, and from the Department of

Commerce that has commercial service officers in a few but, in my view, not enough of the countries?

So sustainability in terms of funding, possibility and value of expanding the number of countries, and then engagement by other agencies, Commerce and Energy.

Mr. GAST. The President, when he launched Power Africa last year, laid out some very ambitious goals; 10,000 megawatts of new power and 20 million new connections. Through careful analysis, we believe that the $285 million that we have as a development agency is sufficient within those six countries to reach those goals. If we are considering expanding the goals, then additional resources would be needed.

With regard to your question about having a line item within the budget, the way that we have treated Presidential initiatives previously is to build it into each country budget with a narrative around how it supports a Presidential initiative. We can certainly look into your request.

Senator COONS. In my view, as I said at the outset and as I think Senator Corker just reflected, sustaining this beyond one administration is a broadly shared goal and could have long-term positive impacts for rural electrification, for the development and deployment of renewables, for addressing I think legitimate environmental concerns about overly focused on generation and in sustaining this reform more broadly.

Senator Flake, any more questions for this panel?

Senator FLAKE. No.

Senator COONS. Senator Markey, we are about to transition to the second panel. If you have a quick question for this first panel——

Senator MARKEY. Thank you so much, Mr. Chairman. And I thank you for having this very important hearing and for allowing me to join the subcommittee today.

It does not quite feel like baseball season yet here in D.C., but I really think the Obama administration is primed to hit a home run here with Power Africa. If we enable Africa with the right technical expertise and financing resources, we are going to see a total revolution in their electricity system and their economy more generally.

And this transformation is going to look a lot different than the way we saw our continent electrified over the last 80 years. The 1936 Congress passed the Rural Electrification Act to fund the massive build-out of transmission lines across the country and to bring electricity from large, mostly coal-fired central power stations to Americans spread out across our Nation. In 1949, that program was amended to similarly build out the wire telephone network.

Africa has, obviously, not followed that path on the telecom front. They skipped the wires. They went straight to mobile technology and the results have been breathtaking. There will be 1 billion mobile subscriptions across the continent in 2015—1 billion. We are talking Africa—1 billion subscriptions. None of that would have been possible in the imaginations of people just 20 years ago.

I was the House author of the Telecommunications Act in 1996. In less than 20 years, that spread to Africa because we passed forward-looking legislation here to think about what was possible in

Africa, in Asia. And we had the hearings on those issues back in the early 1990s, mid-1990s, talking about what was possible, what could our imagination take us to.

The same potential for technological leapfrogging is there with electricity. Instead of spending billions of dollars building huge, polluting central station generators and stringing thousands of miles of transmission lines, there is an opportunity here to build a more decentralized grid that utilizes local renewable resources. And they can do it with American-made technology.

Mimi, do you agree with that? I apologize. I am not going to try to say your—can you say your name for me please?

Ms. ALEMAYEHOU. That is okay. I was already on a first name basis with Senator Flake. [Laughter.]

Senator MARKEY. Excellent. Great minds think alike.

Ms. ALEMAYEHOU. Well, as you know very well, the continent has a huge need, 600 million people in the dark, and so it will require every source of energy.

As you may know, OPIC has had a very, very healthy renewable energy portfolio worldwide but also actually in Africa. Currently in our pipeline, we have wind deals in Kenya. We have solar in Tanzania. We have biofuel in Tanzania. We did a solar deal last year in South Africa. So there is very strong interest from U.S. investors investing in the renewable energy market in the continent.

But as you know, every country in Africa, obviously, is unique. There are some countries like my country of birth, Ethiopia again—I will give an example—where 90 percent of the energy source is hydro, and the other additional would probably come from geothermal. And Kenya and others——

Senator MARKEY. But there is a lot of sun in Ethiopia, as I recall, from my——

Ms. ALEMAYEHOU. Yes. Unless you are there in the summer, yes, there is a lot of sun as well. But geothermal is also very, very cheap. Because they are across the Rift Valley, the whole Kenya, Tanzania, Ethiopia have huge geothermal potential. But countries like obviously Mozambique, which have huge finds in gas as well, will probably develop those kind of energy resources as well.

Senator MARKEY. Let me go to you, Mr. Gast. In your written testimony, you state that Power Africa continues to explore opportunities to bundle together off-grid projects so that institutional investors can deploy capital into these projects at scale. That is a very encouraging thing to hear, but I am quite concerned that we may not be seeing adequate progress in that area. Are you seeing models that work here that we can scale up?

Mr. GAST. Absolutely we are, and if you do not mind, Senator, I will give you an example.

We have a partnership with Cummins Power. They have proprietary technology on biogas. There is an invasive species in the Rift Valley in Baringo County, for example, in Kenya where we are piloting this effort. The invasive species is what we would call mesquite. It is very harmful to the local population and very harmful to their cattle. So we are helping organize communities so that there is a collection effort of this invasive species so that the communities are earning money from this. We have helped Cummins Power and turned to a power purchasing agreement with KPLC.

That is the power and light company of Kenya. The economics are there, and we have one project that is underway and we are looking at replicating it not only throughout Kenya but also into other parts of east Africa.

Senator MARKEY. So I understand that your off-grid program provides loan guarantees for fewer than 30 projects a year worldwide across all sectors. What can be done to increase the number of projects supported in total and to off-grid entrepreneurs in particular beyond the good things that come from bringing clean, reliable power to hundreds of millions of people that do not currently have it?

I think it is also important to highlight how much this program stands to benefit the American economy. The clean energy sector is worth an estimated $2.3 trillion over the next decade. Power Africa will help booster American companies in this huge growth sector. Can you talk about that a little bit, how it helps our country as well?

Mr. GAST. Absolutely. OPIC mobilizes American capital for investment in Africa. Through our development credit authority, we help mobilize local capital. And so local currency is also critical for projects, especially those that are operating at a smaller scale. We have a history of working with banks throughout the country to help with the portfolio guarantees and to increase their confidence that their investments are going to be good investments.

We, in the 2015 bill, have asked for authority to expand that from $1.5 billion to $2 billion, which would allow us to do much more on small-scale renewable and easily replicable projects on the continent.

Senator MARKEY. So next year in Africa, there will be 1 billion people walking around with devices like this, and they are not going to have black rotary dial phones the way we did in America for 80 years. We could not figure out how to get out of that trap, the utility trap, the trap of saying we have to take it from the utility. They are not going to innovate. They are not going to change.

So we have to help these countries to not fall into the same trap because the same potential is there for them for solar, for wind, for other renewable energy resources rather than forcing them to get trapped or financing the trap of having to be tied to the central grid that runs contrary to where all of history and all of technology is now heading not only here but all across the planet, but especially on a continent that can really look at this through fresh eyes. They have done it. They have skipped the wire for one source. They can skip the wire for another.

Thank you, Mr. Chairman.

Senator COONS. Thank you, Senator Markey.

And thank you very much to our first panel. Assistant Administrator Gast, Vice President Alemayehou, and Director Angiuoni, thank you for your testimony and your engagement.

We would like to move, if we can, quickly to our second panel given the limitations of time we face. We have votes in half an hour.

I would like to welcome to the table Tony Elumelu, chairman of Heirs Holdings; and Paul Hinks, CEO of Symbion Power; Del

Renigar, senior counsel for General Electric; and Tom Hart, U.S. executive director of The ONE Campaign.

As we begin our second panel, I would like to specifically thank Mr. Elumelu for traveling from Nigeria to be here with us today and to share with us an African perspective. Your leadership role in advancing Africapitalism and in partnering with Power Africa is particularly welcome and appreciated.

And if we would move in order down the panel, that would be terrific.

Mr. Elumelu.

STATEMENT OF TONY O. ELUMELU, CHAIRMAN OF HEIRS HOLDINGS, FOUNDER OF THE TONY ELUMELU FOUNDATION, LAGOS, NIGERIA

Mr. ELUMELU. Mr. Chairman, I want to thank you, Senator Coons, high Ranking Member Senator Flake, and Senator Markey, for extending this kind invitation to me to make testimony to the subcommittee of the Senate Foreign Relations on this important topic of powering Africa. And I would like to say when Senator Flake called me on Monday to attend this testimony, I was excited to come because of the importance and significance of what you and your committee members are doing. So thank you.

I am the chairman of Heirs Holdings and the founder of the Tony Elumelu Foundation. Heirs Holdings is a pan-African investment company which operates in strategic sectors of the economy, including banking, oil and gas, agribusiness, real estate, and power. We take a long-term investment approach in order to unlock value for our stakeholders and to create a catalytic effect in propelling Africa's economic development.

I coined the term "Africapitalism" to describe our approach to business. I believe that long-term investment in key sectors like power can create economic prosperity and social wealth, benefiting investors and Africa's development future. At its core, Africapitalism has an economic philosophy that encourages practices that create and multiply value locally.

Energy poverty is very close to my heart. I am an entrepreneur, one that is born, raised, and educated in Africa, and through the work of the Tony Elumelu Foundation, we are helping to launch and support a thousand more successful entrepreneurs across the continent. Through our philanthropic efforts, I have repeatedly seen how lack of access to reliable power has constrained human potential and stifled economic growth across the continent.

Currently over 600 million of my fellow Africans have no access to electricity and many more lack reliable access. We are a continent of entrepreneurs, some of the smartest in the world. But how many budding entrepreneurs can really succeed and create more jobs if they do not have lights to power SMEs or the cost of electricity is more than 55 percent of the operating costs of their business? The lack of electricity in sub-Saharan Africa has significant implications on livelihoods. Lack of electricity significantly impairs food security. Technology advancements have supported food security in the West, while the lack of electricity in sub-Saharan Africa has meant that the current population continues to rely on rudimentary facilities for harvesting and storage without the benefit of processing a value addition that could support food security and boost livelihoods.

Lack of electricity impairs national security, too. Because extremism, as you know, is—forever poverty, with only 54 million new jobs available for the 122 million Africans expected to join the workforce by 2020, I am extremely alarmed and concerned with what this means for national security. The creation of jobs in Africa is completely dependent on industry, and industry cannot thrive without a consistent supply of electricity.

Mr. Chairman, the point, therefore, is why is Power Africa Initiative important to Africans, why is what your members are doing very important to Africans. The leadership of the United States is considering this issue at an important time as African citizens from both the public and private spheres are prioritizing the issue of electricity access and linking success in this area to the alleviation of poverty and promotion of lasting economic prosperity. Power Africa, therefore, is a vital important initiative for the following reasons.

First is influence matters. The U.S. Government's elevation of this issue has galvanized both the private sector in the United States and other countries to examine the African power sector as an opportunity for viable investments.

Second, using a coordinated approach, Power Africa set a collective and measurable target to generate an additional 10,000 megawatts within a set timeframe for United States agencies, African governments, the African private sector, and the investors to work toward in Africa.

Third, the establishment of Power Africa has also encouraged other African nations to undertake reforms of their regulatory structures so as to participate in future power deals and partnerships.

In my opinion, Power Africa must by viewed by the administration and this distinguished body as only a start. The initiative is valued at $7 billion, and Africa's infrastructural needs are estimated to be in excess of $300 billion. But like all long journeys, the journey to infrastructure sufficiency in Africa begins with the first step or, in this case, the first $1 billion.

At the request of the leadership of your committee, I would like to say that the African success story I would like to share with you today is that of the Ughelli power plant in Nigeria. This is located in the Niger Delta region of Nigeria. Through Transcorp Limited PLC, Heirs Holdings committed to invest $2.5 billion to generate about 2,000 megawatts of electricity over a 5-year period under the Power Africa Initiative. This represents about 20 percent of the U.S. Government goal of doubling access to electricity in Africa for the same period of time.

The initial investment in the Transcorp Ughelli plant was $300 million from mid last year. When we first took over the plant in November last year, its power output was less than 160 megawatts of power. By January 2014, this year, we had doubled its output to 348 megawatts, and this morning I am happy to say that we have gone up to 382 megawatts of electricity with an ongoing investment of an additional $200 million to refurbish some turbines, we project that we will be generating over 700 megawatts by the end of this year. We are doing this in partnership with one of your own, Symbion Power, who is here also. And General Electric is giving technical support to us also. We are actually again working with both Symbion and General Electric for an additional 1,000 megawatts expansion, which will cost us $1 billion.

I am pleased to inform you that we are on track to fulfill our commitment to Power Africa and we will be producing the equivalent of almost 50 percent of the current total output of 4,200 megawatts in Nigeria today. And in 2015, we will begin plans to generate power in other west African and east African countries.

Transcorp really also currently directly provides employment for nearly 300 full-time workers and 1,000 contractors, and this will grow to 700 employees and 2,000 contractors with the planned additional 1,000 expansion. And we have not even calculated the thousands of tangential and consequential jobs that we created by the plant and the output.

Mr. Chairman, let me say a few words on a topic that has been discussed already this morning, and that is natural gas, climate change, and environmental sustainability.

With respect to climate change, environmental sustainability, and concerns about the development of natural gas for power, our company, Heirs Holdings, believes strongly in protecting the environment for future generations. But we also recognize the importance of addressing the other needs of this generation. Through a mix of renewable and nonrenewable resources, in accordance with the African country plans, some of whom prioritize the abundantly available natural gas resources, to follow up with this in context, the annual average carbon emission in sub-Saharan African countries is .3 tons per person. In Europe, the average is 10 tons per person. And in the United States, average annual emissions are as high as 17 tons per person. Africans now want to harness these same resources that abundantly exist on the continent to meet our own urgent development needs. Sub-Saharan African countries account for less than 3 percent of total global carbon emissions—our progress via—of the climate change problem, and it simply cannot be solved on the backs of these people.

Finally, Mr. Chairman, we call our company Heirs Holdings because we are committed to enhancing the lives of Africans today and driven to create transformative change for future generations in Africa. We believe in Africa. We believe in our ability to help catalyze its emergence as a strong player in the global economy, and we are confident that history will remember who played a role in making this happen. And that is why this committee and what this Government is doing will be remembered not just by this generation of Africa but future generations of Africa will remember those who made it possible or played a role in improving access to electricity.

Thank you again, Mr. Chairman and Senator Flake, for your kind invitation to participate in this important hearing, and I look forward to answering your questions.

[The prepared statement of Mr. Elumelu follows:]

PREPARED STATEMENT OF TONY O. ELUMELU

Good morning. I want to begin by thanking Chairman Coons and Ranking Member Flake for inviting me to testify before this committee and provide an African private sector perspective on President Obama's Power Africa Initiative. More importantly, thank you for your leadership in holding this hearing on a very important issue that has a profound daily impact on the lives hundreds of millions of people in Africa.

HEIRS HOLDINGS AND OUR FOUNDATIONAL PHILOSOPHY OF AFRICAPITALISM

I am the Chairman of Heirs Holdings and founder of the Tony Elumelu Foundation. Heirs Holdings is a Pan-African investment company head quartered in Lagos, Nigeria, which operates in strategic sectors of industry including banking, hospitality, agribusiness, health care, power and energy. We take a long-term view in order to unlock value for our shareholders and to have a catalytic effect in propelling Africa's economic development.

We have coined the phrase ''Africapitalism'' to describe our approach to business—our belief that long-term investment in key sectors, like power, can create economic prosperity and social wealth, benefiting investors and Africa's development future. At its core, Africapitalism is an economic philosophy that seeks to encourage practices that create, retain, and multiply value locally. This is critical to stimulating and sustaining job creation and economic growth.

THE CHALLENGE OF ELECTRICITY ACCESS—THE LOSS OF HUMAN POTENTIAL

We are all familiar with the statistics:

- Nearly 600 million, or 7 out of 10, Africans have no access to electricity;
- Only 2 percent of South Sudanese and Burundians, and 3 percent of Liberians, have access to electricity. In my country of Nigeria, half of the population lives in total darkness, and those who do have electricity have unreliable access;
- In African Business Enterprise surveys, more than 50 percent of businesses cited lack of electricity as a major constraint to their growth.

This is happening at a time when half of Africa's 200 million people are between the ages of 15 and 24, a potential boom or bomb, and we need to create 13 million jobs per year to absorb them.

It is also important to note that many of the greatest, and solvable, health challenges in Africa, which are priorities for U.S. foreign assistance, are linked to energy poverty of the people and government agencies that provide basic health services.

- An estimated 4 million deaths per year, globally, are associated from illnesses derived from cooking with wood and charcoal.
- Millions of child mortalities can be linked to lack of cold chains needed to distribute vaccines.
- Blood supplies cannot be properly tested and preserved to save lives.
- Similarly, millions of mothers and babies are lost every year from lack of power-driven diagnostic and surgical interventions.
- Laboratories cannot function regularly and effectively.

Education is another fundamental sector necessary for achieving development gains, yet 90 million children go to school without electricity. This translates to millions of lost hours of study and homework every day. Over time, this will become a cumulatively unrecoverable loss for a continent with a large youth population, who will lack the necessary understanding and skills to power the continent's industries, and to emerge as a full player in an integrated global economy. This large and expanding pool of unskilled labor would condemn the continent to a continued role as an extractives source—the source of energy, food, and raw materials for use by other world regions—while its own citizens lack the ability to access and benefit from their own abundant resources.

In short, if we can fix power, we can transform lives, and we can realize our potential as an emergent continent.

THE POWER AFRICA INITIATIVE

Many African countries had already begun to prioritize and address their electricity-access needs before President Obama's announcement of the Power Africa Initiative, during his July 2013 trip to the continent, so local ownership and local momentum were in place.

Nigeria's privatization process was already under way, just as it was in countries like Tanzania and Ghana. In fact, with the exception of Liberia, given its post conflict status, most of the countries selected to participate were partly chosen on the basis of the reforms already enacted by their governments in the power sector.

The above being said, there is no substitute for the power of the American Presidency and the U.S. Congress in setting the global agenda and global priorities. I view the initiative as a precedent setting engagement on the continent, one that offers Africans an opportunity to be partners and not dependents. More specifically:

- First, influence matters. As the global leader, when the U.S. Government pays attention to an issue, the world pays attention too. The U.S. Government's elevation of this issue, and coordinated approach to tackling it, has galvanized the private sector in the U.S., and other countries, to examine the African power sector as an opportunity for viable investments.
- Second, Power Africa created a collective and measurable target of 10,000 MW, within a set timeframe, for U.S. agencies, African governments, the African private sector, and outside investors to work toward.
- Third, the establishment of Power Africa has also encouraged other Africa nations beyond the "Power Six" to seek U.S. assistance to undertake reforms of their regulatory structures, so as not to miss opportunities to participate in future power deals and partnerships.
- Most African countries are natural allies for American business. Many of our citizens were educated in the U.S., our professionals gained experience here, hundreds of millions of us speak English as you do, our financial, regulatory, and business practices are similar to, or based on, yours, and millions of our citizens were born or live here in the U.S. It is a long overdue effort for the U.S. Government to help find a way for these African diasporans to engage in economic activities within the framework of a mutually beneficial bilateral partnership.

All of the above being said, Power Africa must be viewed by this administration and this distinguished body as only a start. The initiative is valued at $7 billion and Africa's infrastructural needs are estimated to be $300 billion. But like all long journeys, the journey to infrastructure sufficiency begins with the first step or, in this case, the first $1 billion.

POWER AFRICA AND THE TRANSCORP UGHELLI POWER PLANT

The success story of power expansion I'd like to share with you today is one of partnership between the U.S. and the African private sector. It is that of the Ughelli plant in the Delta region of Nigeria. Heirs Holdings pledged to commit to the Power Africa Initiative because we felt it was important to support the innovative approach to development being undertaken by the American Government. We also felt it was important for the African private sector to step up to the plate and be part of the development effort on the continent, in a way that is consistent with our mission to create value for our shareholders.

Our Power Africa commitment was to invest up to $2.5 billion to generate 2,000 MW of electricity over 5 years, toward President Obama's goal of doubling access to electricity in Africa over the same period. Heirs acquired the Ughelli power plant as part of the Nigerian Government's privatization of the power sector. When we took over the plant in November, it had never produced more than 160 megawatts (MW) of power. By January 1, 2014, we had doubled its output to 348MW and project that we will be generating 725 MW by the end of the year. We are also beginning a rehabilitation of the turbines in the plant and an expansion, to generate an additional 1,000 MW at Ughelli.

I am pleased to report that we are on track to fulfill our commitment to Power Africa and we will be producing more than one-third of the total current output in Nigeria which is 5,898 MW. And our power investments will not be limited to Nigeria. In 2015, we will begin to roll out our plans to generate power in other West and East African countries.

We are meeting these objectives, working with America partners. Symbion, a U.S. power company, led by my friend, Paul Hinks, who is also testifying today, is one of our investors in Ughelli. General Electric (GE), the world's foremost leader in power technology provided us with technical expertise to help increase the output of the plant, and we're in talks to work together on the Ughelli rehabilitation and expansion. Encouraging and supporting these types of partnerships between African and U.S. companies is one of the major contributions of Power Africa.

Ughelli currently directly provides employment for nearly 300 full-time workers and 1,000 contractors, and this will grow to 700 employees and 2,000 contractors with the expansion. We cannot yet estimate the number of jobs that will indirectly be created because new and existing businesses will have increased access to power.

CONCERNS AROUND THE EXPLOITATION OF NATURAL GAS TO EXPAND ELECTRICITY ACCESS IN SOME AFRICAN COUNTRIES

There is some debate around how Africa ramps up its energy use and what resources it will utilize. Africa has tremendous energy potential, via both renewable and nonrenewable resources, and most countries have fully developed national plans and priorities around their existing energy resources. Many are interested in hydro, geothermal, solar and wind power, with the latter two of particular interest in providing off-grid solutions for rural dwellers.

Additionally, natural gas is abundantly available in several African countries, to the tune of billions of cubic meters. Only 15 percent of Mozambique's population has access to electricity, yet the country may possess up to 150 trillion cubic meters of natural gas. With 180 trillion cubic meters of gas, Nigeria actually has more gas than oil. For the last 3 decades, companies have flared this gas, amounting to roughly 1.2 billion cubic feet daily in wasted energy, sending it into the atmosphere, harming the health of local populations and negatively impacting the environment. Today, along with hydropower, Nigeria's national energy plan prioritizes the harnessing of its trillions of cubic meters of natural gas reserves, to help stabilize its current grid and increase energy access for our millions of citizens who still lack regular access to power.

Working within the national energy plan, Transcorp, a subsidiary of Heirs Holdings, made the strategic investment in the Ughelli gas plant, thereby helping to reduce gas flaring and carbon emissions. Transcorp also just concluded another round of Environmental and Social Impact Assessment (ESIA) for the plant, with an aim of ensuring that we manage the environment around our plant in a responsible manner. The earlier mentioned plans to rehabilitate our turbines will also help to reduce carbon emissions, while transforming the lives of our people.

Some stakeholders resist any use of natural gas over concerns about the climate change impact. The Heirs group of companies care strongly about protecting the environment for future generations, but we also recognize the importance of addressing the urgent needs of this generation. As I explained earlier, energy poverty is a pressing concern which impacts many social development indicators.

To further put this in context, the average annual carbon emissions in sub-Saharan African countries is .8 metric tons per capita. The average for the European Union is over 7 metric tons per capita, and in the United States, average annual emissions are as high as 17 metric tons per capita. And every day millions of barrels of oil and gas leave the continent to be used by more developed countries to satisfy their own energy needs. Africans now want to harness these same resources to meet our own urgent development needs.

We must not look at this situation in stark black and white terms, but recognize that we are all stakeholders in developing the continent in a sustainable way. We can do this by encouraging energy efficiencies and clean technologies and by working with each nation to develop a national plan for the harnessing and preservation of its natural resources.

CONCLUSION AND RECOMMENDATIONS

Introduce and pass the Electrify Africa Act: Passage before the end of this Congress is critical because it would be historic, and codify the expansion of access to electricity in Africa as a U.S. Government development and foreign policy priority and ensure continuity for the next President and Congress. Like the Africa Growth and Opportunities Act (AGOA), Power Africa, augmented by Electrify Africa Act, has the ability to help lay the foundations for a new U.S.-Africa relationship: one based on partnership for mutual economic benefit, which simultaneously delivers development gains through capacity-building, technology and knowledge transfer, and regulatory reform.

Take long-term approach to development policymaking in Africa, particularly in the power sector: It is all about de-risking the sector and supporting those partnering for a collective benefit. Not only do investors need the predictability and assurance of a continuity of policy and flow of financing, but it takes a long time to put the infrastructure in place to realize their return on investments.

Look at development differently: Multilateral and bilateral development agencies, like the African Development Bank, also need to consider prioritizing the provision of funds to create sovereign guarantees, bond securitization, and other ways of de-risking the sector with the clear objective of facilitating private investment in power. Funds could be pooled and reprogrammed for this purpose. Similarly, development finance institutions need to be unleashed to provide support to sustainable and responsible investment in the power sector.

Incentivize policy reforms and energy efficiencies through programmatic support to governments and institutions: There is no amount of capital investment or entrepreneurial zeal that will provide affordable and sustainable access to electricity for Africa's 1.5 billion people without the full buy-in and energetic support of African governments. With the best of intentions, for more than 30 years, the various Nigerian military and civilian governments could not come close to meeting the energy needs of their citizens. However, when the current government worked in collaboration with the private sector to develop a sensible privatization plan and schedule, the private sector stepped up to the plate. The government also incentivized the long-term investment required for the power sector by instituting the multiyear tariff order to ensure that investors in the power sector earn an attractive rate of return on their investment.

Make strategic investments in catalytic and transformative sectors by taking a supply chain approach to your development policy: Heirs did not start out intending to go into power, our goal was to break into the oil and gas sector as a domestic producer. However, with a lot of gas reserves within our assets and recognizing the needs in our country for electricity, we proceeded to invest in converting that gas to electricity. We are also looking down the supply chain and exploring opportunities for power distribution to tackle power from raw material to end consumption. Basically, we plan to go from our oil and gas block to serving our neighborhood blocks.

Make engagement with the African private sector a congressional priority in oversight and new policymaking: Public-private partnerships are critical to developing the African Continent, particularly in the power sector. It is important to recognize the revolution that has taken place in the African private sector and that we've stepped up to the development plate.

CONCLUSION

We call our company Heirs Holdings because we are committed to enhancing the lives of Africans today, but driven to create transformative change for future generations.

Despite all of these hardships the continent is home to 7 of the 10 fastest-growing economies in the world. According to UNCTAD's 2013 Global Investment Report, at an average of 9.3 percent, Africa offers the highest rate of return on investment of any region in the world and 26 African countries have committed to support the goal of providing universal energy access by 2030.

Imagine the potential that could be unleashed if we get electricity right. Imagine the GDP growth, the education, and job opportunities for our youth and the families lifted out of poverty. Imagine Africa's future.

Thank you again for your kind invitation to participate in this important hearing, and I look forward to answering your questions.

Senator COONS. Thank you, Mr. Elumelu.

Mr. Renigar.

STATEMENT OF DEL RENIGAR, SENIOR COUNSEL FOR GLOBAL GOVERNMENT AFFAIRS AND POLICY, GENERAL ELECTRIC, WASHINGTON, DC

Mr. RENIGAR. Mr. Chairman, Ranking Member Flake, members of the subcommittee, it is a pleasure to be here today.

I am Del Renigar with General Electric. General Electric is the world's largest infrastructure company. We like to tackle the world's toughest challenges finding solutions across health care, home, finance, energy, and transportation, and nowhere in the world is that more relevant than sub-Saharan Africa. We have been in sub-Saharan Africa since 1898, started in South Africa, but have transformed our operations across the continent, across 35 countries. We now employ over 1,800 people in sub-Saharan Africa, and sub-Saharan Africa is a strategic focus for our company. Our headquarters are in Nairobi, Kenya, and we continue to see huge opportunities for growth.

Power Africa is a fantastic initiative that is fully supported by GE. We committed to help bring online at least 5,000 megawatts, and we believe we are making very solid progress in achieving that target.

Power Africa is a great approach. We believe the whole-of-government focus, as well as the coordination with the in-country team and the transaction advisors, is a really smart way to go. Senator Flake, I am sure you are focused on basketball this time of the year. It is really the perfect high-low kind of approach and we see tremendous progress and results because of that coordination and the reach-back to Washington.

We have been very active in a number of projects already. We are doing gas projects in Nigeria and Tanzania and Ghana. We are doing wind projects in Kenya. We also see opportunities to do more wind in Ethiopia.

There has been a lot of talk about off-grid and distributed power. We are very engaged on those topics. As has been mentioned, we put together this off-grid challenge with the U.S.-African Development Foundation to encourage African innovators and entrepreneurs to come up with smart ideas for off-grid and renewable solutions.

At the same time, though, I cannot help but comment that the gas issues are really central to this. Africa has tremendous gas resources and we need to figure out ways to deploy those resources to improve the quality of life on the continent.

I want to focus, Mr. Chairman, on your priorities and how do we institutionalize this. I think there are a few things that we can be doing and we are already starting to see some progress on this.

Number one, it is really standardizing documents and templates. There ought to be a standard model for PPA's, a standard model for IPP's, a standard way of providing credit enhancements for off-takers. That can be replicated, then banked for projects across the continent.

We believe there needs to be an intense focus on gas to power. One of the most frustrating things in sub-Saharan Africa is you have all this gas and no way to translate it into power. We need to be focusing on the infrastructure that can provide that gas to those power locations. Even distributed power runs on gas. It is not all renewables. Gas is a central feature of distributed power. We need to be looking at pricing. We need to be looking at subsidies. We need to be looking at allocation of gas to meet the target of doubling access.

We also need to be looking at grid capacity. If you are going to bring on this many renewables and this much gas, you have to look at whether the grid can stabilize and what improvements, what management techniques can be brought to bear on the grid.

Finally, biogas. You heard from USAID this is an area where we believe that there needs to be a policy focus on providing more incentives and more of a framework on how to encourage countries to go after this. We think Ethiopia and Tanzania are places where we could also see huge progress on biogas.

Finally, Mr. Chairman, you asked about what the Congress can do. The Congress, of course, can do a lot. Reauthorizing Ex-Im Bank and OPIC is critical. Sixty percent of GE's revenues now come from outside the United States. That means to sustain our manufacturing base in this country, we need help from Ex-Im Bank and OPIC.

We also believe USAID's development credit authority is a great tool for encouraging U.S. exports and engagement with the world.

Finally, I want to touch specifically on the carbon cap issue and the Electrify Africa Act. We are strong supporters of the Electrify Africa Act. However, we do believe there needs to be a focus on the carbon cap issue. The omnibus has provided one solution, but we think a permanent solution is appropriate here.

Finally, we continue to support more commercial resources from the Commerce Department on the continent to provide that market intelligence and that support.

Thank you again for this opportunity. I look forward to your questions.

[The prepared statement of Mr. Renigar follows:]

PREPARED STATEMENT OF DEL RENIGAR

Mr. Chairman, Ranking Member Flake, and members of the subcommittee, thank you for the opportunity to testify today on the Power Africa Initiative. I am Del Renigar, Senior Counsel for Global Government Affairs and Policy, for General Electric.

As you know, sub-Saharan Africa is home to tremendous people and tremendous resources. Yet, sub-Saharan Africa is mired in energy poverty:

- Sub-Saharan Africa accounts for only 12 percent of the global population, but almost 45 percent of those are without basic access to electricity.
- Nearly 7 out of every 10 Africans still have no access to what we would consider modern electricity.
- 90 million sub-Saharan children have no electricity at school.
- 70 percent of businesses cite the lack of access to reliable power as a major constraint.
- 225 million sub-Saharans rely on health facilities that are without electricity.

At GE, we believe that power has the potential to transform lives and communities and bring economic growth to every corner of the globe, especially sub-Saharan Africa. Through our presence in sub-Saharan Africa, we directly witness how the continent's power deficit impacts every element of daily life and work, with pronounced impacts in education, public health, medical care, and business productivity. We are enthusiastic partners with the U.S. Government in launching and implementing the Power Africa Initiative, which we see as a new framework for public-private collaboration to address some of the world's most intractable challenges.

BACKGROUND

GE is the world's largest infrastructure company. We bring the best people and the best technologies to take on the toughest challenges, finding solutions in energy, health and home, transportation and finance. GE has been actively involved in Africa for well over a century. The Company established the South African General Electric Company in 1898, and has been a reliable partner to African nations and communities since that time. We now have more than 1,800 employees working across 35 countries in the region, providing solutions and services that support Africa's infrastructure and sustainable growth.

We have a strong foundation for serving as a partner to the U.S. Government (USG) in implementing the Power Africa Initiative. Several GE business units contribute to serving Africa's energy needs, but the principal technology and service provider for Power Africa is GE's Power & Water business, which provides customers with a broad array of power generation, energy delivery, and water process technologies to solve their challenges locally. Power & Water works across the spectrum of fuel sources, including renewable resources such as wind and solar; biogas and alternative fuels; natural gas; coal; oil and nuclear energy. Headquartered in Schenectady, NY, Power & Water is GE's largest industrial business.

POWER AFRICA INITIATIVE

GE is one of the founding private sector partners for the Power Africa Initiative. At the project announcement in June 2013, we committed to help bring online 5,000 megawatts of new electric generation capacity, in cooperation with the Initiative's government and other private sector partners. We are proud to join these partners in alleviating sub-Saharan Africa's most significant development challenge and laying the foundation for Africa's economies to prosper and the health, well-being, safety, and productivity of its people to flourish.

One of the important strengths of Power Africa is that it brings a whole-of-government approach and focuses it on a single metric: doubling access to power in sub-Saharan Africa. In pursuing that goal, Power Africa has the potential to address some of the longstanding policy and regulatory bottlenecks to solving Africa's power problem. It also provides a unique opportunity to support Africa in developing new energy resources that provide an unparalleled opportunity to accelerate access to power—including natural gas and renewables. By operating at the policy level, Power Africa can enable the development of a clear framework to incentivize investment in sustainable power for the long term. By operating at the transactional level, Power Africa can help get deals done. The obstacles in developing and executing these energy projects are complex and multifaceted, ranging from securing financing to obtaining regulatory approval to negotiating with local utilities and off-takers. The coordinated, interagency nature of Power Africa provides the type of cross-cutting support that enables power projects to move forward.

Power Africa's on-the-ground coordination out of Nairobi and its placement of embedded in-country advisors in the African ministries complements the ''whole-of-government'' approach. This lends a strong, local perspective and understanding to the administration of the Initiative and enhances the awareness and capabilities of the local ministries combined with domain and process expertise in Washington.

Because the GE Africa team is able to meet regularly with the on-the-ground USG team and share information in real time with interagency partners, we can all act quickly from multiple angles on multiple fronts to keep projects on track. For example, the GE, USG and Kenyan Government teams were activated in a matter of hours on both sides of the ocean when Kenya considered tariffs that would have increased the cost of wind projects.

GE PROJECTS AND INVESTMENTS

GE is pursuing a range of projects and technologies to support its commitment to the Power Africa Initiative. Local needs vary drastically across and even within the Power Africa countries, and each requires a solution tailored to that context. We are using expertise across the full spectrum of fuel sources, including natural gas, wind, and other renewables like biogas, to meet these needs in a way that is suitable in each context. Grid capacity and connectivity is a huge challenge in many parts of the region, and we are also supporting a portfolio of grid-based and off-grid solutions with our specialized expertise in distributed power. While many projects are still in various stages of planning, financing, and implementation, I would like to highlight several major accomplishments below.

Natural Gas

One of our most significant efforts to date has been focused on the privatization of the Nigerian power sector. This effort is focused on improving performance at existing generation and distribution assets, and adding additional capacity going forward. Power Africa's advisors in Nigeria have supported capacity-building in the Nigeria power sector, including through advising on power privatization in the Bureau of Public Enterprises. As independent and neutral advisors, the Power Africa advisors have worked with the Nigerian authorities to develop the Power Purchase Agreement (PPA) for the Nigeria Bulk Electricity Trader (NBET). This included an innovative put/call structure that helped to enhance the creditworthiness of the NBET as the final off-taker and provide developers with recourse in the event of default. If adopted, this will provide a model for PPAs in Nigeria and reduce the obstacles to concluding negotiations on power generation projects. Indeed, innovative ways of enhancing off-taker credit should be explored throughout the other Power Africa countries as well.

We have also made significant progress in developing gas power projects in Tanzania, where we expect to bring the Kinyerezi-Tanesco 150 megawatt project on line this year. Ghana also offers the opportunity to bring significant new power on line with the development of major gas-fired power projects. In particular, the Ghana 1000 project aims to bring on line 1,000 megawatts of power over the next 6 years. In June of last year, GE signed an MOU with the Ghanaian Government and established a consortium of companies to fast track fuel availability through the global LNG supply and to create options for gas capacity to support other projects.

Power Africa, working along with the Millennium Challenge Corporation (MCC), has the opportunity to support the transformation of Ghana's power sector by supporting LNG infrastructure. We also believe that Ex-Im and OPIC are potential sources of financing for the projects. If MCC, Ex-Im, OPIC and the other Power Africa agencies were to engage across the entire value chain of the Ghana 1000 project including fuel supply, infrastructure, incentives and execution, then Power Africa could demonstrate an ability to support end-to-end development of innovative, large-scale energy sector transformations.

Wind

We are actively supporting the Kenyan Government's objective to increase the country's power capacity by an additional 5,000 megawatts. We are involved in two major wind projects, including supplying turbines to the 60 megawatt Kinangop Wind Project, which reached financial close in late 2013. The project is scheduled to start construction this year. We also expect to see significant progress this year on the Kipeto Wind Project, which would ultimately produce an additional 100 megawatts.

We also see significant wind opportunities in Ethiopia.

Off-Grid Energy Challenge

At GE, innovation is at the heart of everything we do, and solutions that drive progress should be elevated and taken seriously—no matter where they come from. African innovators and entrepreneurs are developing new technologies to tackle the continent's energy deficit, and we are determined to lend scale and resources to these transformative ideas that have the potential to solve this challenge. We recently announced the first round of winners of the Power Africa Off-Grid Energy Challenge, which we are sponsoring in conjunction with the U.S. African Development Foundation. We solicited the best ideas from African entrepreneurs and innovators designing innovative off-grid energy solutions that deploy renewable resources and support local economic activity. Winners from Kenya and Nigeria designed innovative projects including solar-powered water points, stand-alone cold storage facilities, urban biodigesters and solar mini-grids. We are looking forward to expanding the program over the coming years.

INSTITUTIONALIZING PROGRESS

Mr. Chairman, we applaud your focus on ensuring that the Power Africa Initiative is institutionalized and continues to achieve important gains for decades to come. We agree wholeheartedly, and we believe there are systematic, structural improvements that would ensure the durability and longevity of the initiative. We also encourage ongoing congressional support for key USG activities that facilitate power projects as a component of broader foreign policy, security, environment and development objectives in the developing world that stress strong private sector participation.

Power Africa Reforms

Our most significant challenges continue to be in three key areas: speed of contracting and financial close; transforming abundant gas resources to power generation; and financing—particularly credit enhancement for off-takers. While Power Africa transaction advisors are doing a good job of advancing individual transactions, we see cross-cutting opportunities to get projects across the finish line more quickly and efficiently. These opportunities include:

- Support effective contracting structures: We constantly face a challenge in navigating contracting structures in a way that provides confidence to financing partners. We believe that the Nigeria PPA can serve as a potential model for other power generation projects in the region. We suggest that Power Africa consider standardizing documentation for IPPs and support credit enhancement for off-takers, with a view toward medium-term creditworthiness. This could significantly speed project implementation. We understand that USAID and the Commerce Department's Commercial Law Development Program are convening private sector experts to develop model templates that can be replicated and banked quickly for projects across sub-Saharan Africa. We support this initiative and believe it can play an important role in facilitating and streamlining the project development process.
- Establish framework for gas-to-power: The mismatch between gas resources and power deficits is one of the most frustrating aspects of working in Africa. This structural issue is orders of magnitude larger and more challenging than any

individual project in Nigeria or Tanzania. We recommend that the Power Africa Initiative create a comprehensive framework to promote gas-to-power in the region, which would examine infrastructure needs for gas networks, gas pricing and allocation, implications for power tariffs and support for alternative solutions that enable power to be provided in remote locations.

- Assess grid capacity: Grid capacity limitations currently act as a constraint to bringing on additional power in many countries. As we make long-term plans for power generation solutions, we recommend that Power Africa undertake a review of grid needs to absorb higher capacity and efficiency equipment. This will facilitate effective planning that matches the most appropriate power resource technology with localized needs and capabilities. This analysis is particularly important as countries introduce a range of generation sources (including renewables, gas, etc.), which produces some instability and requires more sophisticated grid management technology and planning.
- Facilitate biogas projects: We see significant potential for biogas-based power generation projects in Africa. These distributed power systems offer win-win solutions for rural communities—they improve waste management practices, avoid greenhouse gas emissions and meet near-term energy needs. While several existing programs support biogas projects, current efforts tend to be one-off, opportunistic solutions. Larger projects still face significant hurdles in achieving commercial viability. We suggest that Power Africa explore more systematic options for reducing costs of project feasibility, in order to enable more significant investments in biogas projects in the region. In particular, we believe that Ethiopia and Tanzania are rich environments for biogas and should be the focus of feasibility studies and pilot projects. Power Africa should examine, for example, whether the USTDA- and OPIC-supported U.S.-Africa Clean Energy Finance Initiative could be a useful tool here.

Congressional Support

Coupled with these programmatic efforts and ongoing oversight, we encourage Congress to continue to support, expand, and improve the core federal programs that enable U.S. companies to meet the needs of foreign markets. At GE, nearly 60 percent of our revenues derive from markets abroad—up from 40 percent just a decade ago—which sustain our domestic manufacturing base. Much of our opportunity for future growth lies in these expanding markets.

We support reauthorizing the Overseas Private Investment Corporation (OPIC) and the Export-Import Bank (Ex-Im), and we encourage Congress to seek improvements to make both institutions more flexible and user-friendly, and to use the full range of their tools and authorities. Similarly, it is important to ensure that the U.S. Agency for International Development (USAID) has sufficient funding and flexibility to use its delegated credit authority to work with companies on projects. We also support efforts led by several members of this committee to ensure sufficient Commerce Department resources for commercial, advocacy, and market intelligence support in sub-Saharan Africa.

In addition, we have been working closely with this committee and your counterparts in the House on the Electrify Africa Act. We believe that the legislation is an important component of a long-term strategy to institutionalize the Power Africa Initiative. We appreciate your commitment to this legislation, and we look forward to continuing to work with you and your staff as a bill is introduced and advanced here in the Senate.

I would like to address one specific issue we have raised as part of the Electrify Africa Act discussion. Until the passage of the FY14 omnibus, the OPIC carbon cap effectively precluded OPIC activity in support of U.S. participation in much of the global energy sector (with the exception of renewable energy projects). Without access to OPIC financing, some projects were delayed or canceled outright, while others were awarded to foreign entities that were able to obtain financing from OPIC-like institutions abroad.

The carbon cap policy hurt U.S. manufacturers of power generation equipment, limited U.S. foreign policy objectives in key regions, constrained the private sector's ability to invest and hampered the developing world's ability to grow and obtain access to basic services, such as electricity. We believe that OPIC can help to meet the urgent demand for increased generation in low-income countries while preserving the integrity of U.S. environmental objectives. The omnibus, which temporarily lifted the carbon cap under certain circumstances, was a step in the right direction. We encourage this committee to consider modifying OPIC's carbon policy on a more permanent basis to enable limited financing and support for power projects for the world's poorest countries.

CONCLUSION

Thank you for the opportunity to share GE's perspective on the Power Africa Initiative. We believe this coordinated, whole-of-government approach offers an innovative and effective mechanism for working with the private sector to address the energy deficit in sub-Saharan Africa. We have seen important successes to date, and we look forward to continuing to work with Initiative leaders to drive even more significant impacts going forward. I appreciate this committee's attention to this critically important Initiative, and I am happy to answer any questions you may have. Thank you.

Senator COONS. Thank you, Mr. Renigar.

I am just going to remind everyone we have votes scheduled at noon. So we are likely to end at noon.

Mr. Hart.

STATEMENT OF TOM HART, U.S. EXECUTIVE DIRECTOR, THE ONE CAMPAIGN, WASHINGTON, DC

Mr. HART. Great. I will try to be brief.

Thank you, Mr. Chairman, so much for inviting me to testify this morning.

The ONE Campaign is an organization committed to the fight against global poverty and disease mostly in Africa. We are probably best known for our cofounder and lead singer of U2, Bono. But with our nearly 2 million members in the United States, we raise attention about critical issues and work with policymakers on bipartisan solutions.

So given our focus on fighting poverty and disease, our interest in energy might seem curious. But the lack of energy impacts nearly all aspects of human development, including health, agriculture, education, and poverty reduction.

And the scope of the problem in Africa is massive, as has been noted a number of times. Seven in ten people in sub-Saharan Africa lack access to modern energy resources, and that grows to 85 percent in rural areas.

African business leaders cite the lack of electricity as a top concern to economic growth and job creation. This deficit is estimated to cost African countries 2 to 5 percent of GDP.

And at a human level, without electricity, mothers give birth by candlelight or must bring their own can of diesel fuel with them to power hospital generators. Many children's vaccines can spoil without refrigeration. Farmers cannot irrigate their fields or store crops. School children often crowd around street lamps at night to study for exams.

For a small farmer in Ethiopia, what difference would cool storage make in keeping her hard-earned crop from spoiling in the heat on the way to market?

For a furnituremaker in Kenya working by hand, what difference would a power saw and a lathe make to growing his small business?

For a mother in Nigeria, what difference would an electric stove and lighting mean to making a meal or heating her family's home? Today she probably burns wood or dung or kerosene. And shockingly, each year more than 3 million people worldwide die prematurely from inhaling toxic smoke from indoor fires and kerosene used for cooking, heating, and lighting. Three million. That is more deaths than from AIDS and malaria combined. As a career-long advocate in the fight against AIDS and malaria, this fact made me realize I could not not work on this issue.

So we are deeply grateful to President Obama and his administration for the Power Africa Initiative which is taking the first serious steps in six African countries toward tackling this disparity.

I am also thrilled that in the House, Chairman Royce and Ranking Member Engel have introduced and cleared through their committee the bipartisan Electrify Africa Act. This would catalyze investments to nearly double the amount of electricity available in sub-Saharan Africa, excluding South Africa, and reach 50 million people with first-time access. And because this bill draws on existing resources in the Government and leverages in private sector capital, these goals can be reached at no additional cost to taxpayers. In fact, the CBO has scored the House bill as a net moneymaker for the United States.

Mr. Chairman, let me also thank you and Chairman Menendez and Senator Corker for considering similar legislation here in the Senate and I look forward to its speedy introduction.

So why is legislation important? Simply put, legislation creates the stability, direction, and support, giving longevity beyond the current administration. I can best relate this to PEPFAR, the United States flagship program to fight HIV/AIDS. President Bush is rightly credited for leading the initiative, but it was built on the shoulders of bipartisan legislation from this body introduced by Senators Frist and Kerry. The legislation was not easy to pass, but it has since been reauthorized twice, maintained strong bipartisan support for a decade, and so far put 7 million people on lifesaving treatment.

Addressing the energy deficit in Africa is earning the same kind of bipartisan support on both ends of Pennsylvania Avenue and, with sustained support through legislation, we believe will be every bit as transformative as PEPFAR has been to the people on the continent of Africa.

Two quick points in conclusion. The people of Africa must be in the driver's seat in terms of the mix of power sources. The good news is African countries are harnessing what they already have in abundance—solar, wind, geothermal, hydro, natural gas—resulting in a mix far more sustainable than we have in the United States. For example, in rural communities, off-grid and mini-grid renewable power is often more viable than traditional grid solutions and can provide rapid access to basic services.

Lastly, let us admit challenges still remain. Generating electricity on the one hand is one issue, but it is quite another to sort out how to get it to people, run power lines, sort out domestic regulations, create a customer payment system. We may not have answers to all of these challenges just yet, but recall that when PEPFAR was signed into law, we still had not figured out how to get high-tech drugs to a highly stigmatized disease to the poorest parts of the continent. There is nothing quite like political leadership and the promise of bold progress to incentivize problem-solving.

The world has made dramatic progress in reducing extreme poverty, cutting it in half over the last 20 years, and it is possible—possible—to virtually eliminate it in our lifetimes. But I am reminded each day that African leaders, nurses, farmers, business owners, teachers, and citizens cite electricity as one of their most urgent daily needs and the engine that can drive the economic growth and poverty reduction that we and, most importantly, the people of Africa strive for.

Thank you.

[The prepared statement of Mr. Hart follows:]

PREPARED STATEMENT OF THOMAS H. HART

Thank you, Mr. Chairman and Senator Flake, for this opportunity to address energy access in sub-Saharan Africa. It is a shocking fact that 7 in 10 Africans lack any access to modern energy sources.

The ONE Campaign is a policy advocacy organization committed to the fight against global poverty and disease, particularly in Africa. We are probably best known for our cofounder and the lead singer of U2, Bono. We don't do service on the ground and we don't raise money from the public. With our nearly 2 million members in the United States, we raise attention about critical issues and work with policymakers on bipartisan solutions.

Given our focus on fighting poverty and disease, our interest in energy might seem curious. But we quickly realized this issue impacts nearly all aspects of human development including health, agriculture, education, economic growth, and poverty reduction.

This reality has been made perfectly clear to us by our partners and friends in Africa. The Sub-Saharan Africa Business Enterprise surveys cite Africa's insufficient and unreliable electricity access as the biggest constraint to business growth, impeding job creation. The lack of modern reliable energy access is estimated to cost African countries 2–5 percent of GDP. Twenty six African countries have committed to the goal of providing universal energy access by 2030 under the U.N. Sustainable Energy for All (SE4ALL) Initiative. The African Union has made regional energy access a top priority.

Early last year, 18 African heads of state and ambassadors—alongside policy, political and civil society leaders in the U.S.—signed ONE's ''Open Statement on Electricity in Africa,'' which details the vast impact of the lack of electricity (see Appendix). The letter noted that lack of electricity means that mothers are forced to give birth by candlelight, and that many children's vaccines can be spoiled without refrigeration, given that 60 percent of refrigerators in health clinics in Africa do not have reliable power. Limited access to modern energy services hinders irrigation, agricultural mechanization, and post-harvest storage and processing. Ninety million children go to primary schools without electricity and most students do not have decent lighting to do their homework after sunset. Some are forced to crowd around street lamps or airport runways at night to study for exams. According to a paper from the Center for Global Development, nearly 90 percent of rural Africans and about half of the urban poor in major cities across Africa, like Nairobi and Dakar, have no access to electricity. In fact, more than 700 African-based NGOs have signed similar letters asking for help on providing electricity to their people.

The world has made dramatic progress in reducing extreme poverty over the last 20 years, cutting it in half. And it is possible to virtually end extreme poverty in our lifetime. But electricity is essential to the kind of human well-being and economic growth needed to meet this audacious goal.

For a small farmer in Ethiopia, what difference would cool storage make in preserving her hard-earned crop on the way to market?

For a furniture maker in Kenya working by hand, what difference would a power saw and lathe make to his small business?

For a mother in Nigeria, what difference would an electric stove and lighting mean to making a meal or lighting and heating her family's home? Liberian President Ellen Johnson Sirleaf wrote in a recent Foreign Policy opinion piece: ''In many places without power, women and girls are forced to spend hours each day in the time-consuming task of hunting for fuel and firewood—often a key reason that girls spend less time in school than boys. Women are also disproportionately affected by respiratory illness as a result of indoor air pollution from open fires and kerosene used for cooking, heating, and lighting. Even the simple act of being outdoors becomes fraught with danger for women and girls in some places when the sun goes down and there are no streetlights.''

The respiratory illness noted by President Sirleaf, stemming from inhaling toxic fumes, results in 3 million premature deaths each year worldwide. That is more deaths than from AIDS and malaria combined. As a career-long advocate in the fight against AIDS and malaria, this fact made me realize this issue could not be ignored.

So, we are deeply grateful to President Obama and his administration for the Power Africa Initiative, which has helped shine a spotlight on this issue and taken the first serious steps toward tackling this disparity in six African countries. U.S. Government commitments combined with substantial investment from the private sector has already started to make an impact.

For example, a key milestone was reached in securing financing for Kenya's Lake Turkana Wind Power Project. This project will add an existing 300 megawatts of reliable, low-cost wind energy to Kenya's national grid and is part of Harith General Partner's Power Africa commitment to provide $70 million in financing for wind energy projects in Kenya and $500 million across the African power sector through a new investment fund.

Power Africa is a crucial first step, but Congress has an important role to play. Increasing energy access is a massive, long-term challenge and it will take a long-term commitment to make a real impact. We are very grateful for the bipartisan work being done in Congress to pass legislation that builds on and strengthens the Power Africa Initiative.

In the House, Chairman Royce and Ranking Member Engel's legislation, the Electrify Africa Act, would catalyze investment in the energy sector in Africa, reaching 50 million people with first-time access with 20 gigawatts of new power, which is close to double the amount of usable power in sub-Saharan Africa outside of South Africa. And because the bill uses resources already available within the government, and leverages private sector capital, these goals can be reached without additional appropriations. In fact, the Congressional Budget Office has estimated that the House bill would raise a net $86 million in revenue. In this case, doing good can actually reduce the deficit.

And I want to compliment Senator Coons and his colleagues, Chairman Menendez and Senator Corker, for considering similar legislation and look forward to its introduction in the near future.

ONE is often asked why legislation is necessary. The answer is simple: legislation will give longevity to the initiative, beyond the Obama administration. The scale of the electricity deficit in Africa combined with the complexity of securing financing and generating and distributing power requires a long-term commitment. While I have every confidence the next administration will embrace this idea, Congress creates the stability, direction, and support. Ten years ago, ONE was heavily involved in the passage of The President's Emergency Plan for AIDS Relief, PEPFAR—the largest investment in any global health challenge and responsible for keeping nearly 7 million people alive today. President Bush deserves enormous credit for his commitment and leadership. What is often forgotten is that it was built on the framework of bipartisan legislation from this chamber—sponsored by Senators Frist and Kerry. Once President Bush announced PEPFAR, legislation was debated, with all the arguments, compromises, twists and turns, resulting in a law that has been reauthorized twice and maintained strong, sustained bipartisan support for 10 years. Addressing the energy deficit in Africa is earning the same bipartisan support from both ends of Pennsylvania Avenue and from the American public, and could be every bit as transformative as PEPFAR has been to the lives of people on the continent.

Most importantly, beyond a sustained commitment to increasing investment in the energy sector in Africa from the U.S. Government and private sector, ONE believes the people of Africa must be in the driver's seat in terms of the mix of power solutions most appropriate to their countries. We have to recognize that with current technology, bringing power to those who do not have it will inevitably lead to a small increase in global carbon emissions. The International Energy Agency estimates that bringing a basic level of energy access to all 1.2 billion people globally who need it would increase emissions by about 0.7 percent. In that context, the U.S. Government, international institutions, civil society organizations and policy experts should support those countries to make better choices than we—and most western nations—did in our own drive to bring power to all.

The good news is that many African countries are choosing cleaner, more sustainable forms of energy from renewable sources and natural gas. In fact, what little electricity Africa currently has is 26 percent renewable—more than two times cleaner than what we have in the United States. Many African countries have barely scratched the surface of their renewable energy potential, from solar to wind to geothermal. As renewable energy becomes more available at an affordable cost, we expect to see, and certainly support, significantly more investment in cleaner energy sources. This is particularly true in rural communities where off-grid and mini-grid renewable power is more viable than traditional grid solutions and can provide rapid access to basic services. Natural gas deposits are also abundant in many African countries and will doubtless be harnessed as part of a mix of solutions to tackle the massive need. In everything we do, we need to recognize that we have obligations both to those whose needs demand urgent attention today and to the generation yet to come who will inherit the planet.

A myriad of other substantial challenges exist in delivering electricity to people in Africa. Generating more electricity on the African Continent is one thing, but it is quite another to sort out how to get it to people, run power lines, sort out tricky domestic regulations, subsidies, and create a customer base. ONE does not pretend to have answers to all these challenges. That is one reason we are so pleased to work with the U.S.-based National Rural Electric Cooperative Association. These are the people who got electricity to rural America and they are now active in Africa and are a critical partner in this effort.

When PEPFAR was signed into law in 2003, we still had not figured out all the difficulties of getting high-priced and technical drugs, to combat a highly stigmatized disease, to the most remote parts of Africa. But, there's nothing quite like political leadership and the promise of bold progress to knock down these tough issues. Reforms happen only as a result of crisis or the promise of bold positive change. The Millennium Challenge Corporation is another good example of this phenomenon, where large development compacts have incited domestic reforms, called the "MCC effect." And I should note the MCC, while not a focus in the legislation, is doing terrific work in the energy sector in Africa.

Challenges certainly remain in delivering access to electricity for the first time to millions of Africans. But I am reminded each day that African leaders, hospital workers, farmers, businessowners, teachers and countless ordinary citizens say that reliable electricity is one of their most urgent needs. American constituents have spoken up as well: more than 100,000 people have signed ONE's petition encouraging and applauding this effort. ONE members have sent over 62,000 individual messages to Members of the House and Senate. There is broad, bipartisan support for these issues—and let me thank the committee again for focusing on this critical component to reducing poverty and promoting health and well-being for people in Africa and for the opportunity to address this panel. Thank you.

APPENDIX

Signatures on this statement do not imply endorsement of specific legislation.

OPEN STATEMENT ON ELECTRICITY IN AFRICA

More than 550 million people in sub-Saharan Africa do not have access to electricity. In 30 African countries, endemic power shortages are a way of life. Without a reliable power supply, women give birth in underequipped hospitals, children's vaccines requiring refrigeration are at risk, students are unable to study after dark and routine business transactions become extremely difficult.

One in five Africans cites infrastructure—including electricity—as their most pressing concern. Seven out of ten business leaders across the region say the lack of affordable and reliable power is one of the most important constraints to growth. The absence of modern energy access limits GDP growth in sub-Saharan Africa by an estimated 2 to 5 percent each year. With 14 million sub-Saharan Africans entering the workforce annually, government leaders are facing the political imperative to address critical and growing energy demands.

The good news is sustainable solutions to address Africa's energy poverty can deliver immediate progress as Africa has yet to harness the majority of its energy potential from renewables and natural gas. Countries are increasingly taking the lead with bold plans to develop these resources for their national benefit. We support the more than two dozen African nations that have committed to the goal of providing universal energy access by 2030, so that people living in rural and urban areas are lifted out of poverty and can benefit from strong economic growth. We encourage catalytic support from the U.S. Government and private sector in order to achieve this large scale increase in energy access. Collectively, this partnership can help provide millions of people access to modern energy which, in turn, will energize progress in all areas of human development and self-sufficiency on the continent.

Signed,

Her Excellency Ellen Johnson Sirleaf, President, Republic of Liberia

His Excellency Adebowale Adefuye, Ambassador to the United States, Federal Republic of Nigeria

His Excellency Daniel Ohene Agyekum, Ambassador to the United States, Ghana

His Excellency Blaise Cherif, Ambassador to the United States, Republic of Guinea
His Excellency Daouda Diabaté, Ambassador to the United States, Republic of Cote d'Ivoire
His Excellency Joseph B.C. Foe-Atangana, Ambassador to the United States, Republic of Cameroon
His Excellency Al Maamoun Baba Lamine Keita, Ambassador to the United States, Republic of Mali
His Excellency Silas Lwakabamba, Minister of Infrastructure, Republic of Rwanda
His Excellency Steve D. Matenje, Ambassador to the United States, Republic of Malawi
His Excellency Cheikh Niang, Ambassador to the United States, Republic of Senegal
His Excellency Abednego M. Ntshangase, Ambassador to the United States, Kingdom of Swaziland
His Excellency Cyrille Oguin, Ambassador to the United States, Republic of Benin
His Excellency E. Molapi Sebatane, Ambassador to the United States, Kingdom of Lesotho
His Excellency Seydou Bouda, Ambassador to the United States, Burkina Faso
His Excellency Bockari Kortu Stevens, Ambassador to the United States, Sierra Leone
His Excellency Jeremiah Congbeh Sulunteh, Ambassador to the United States, Republic of Liberia
Her Excellency Maria De Fátima Lima da Veiga, Ambassador to the United States, Republic of Cape Verde
His Excellency Oliver Wonekha, Ambassador to the United States, Republic of Uganda
African Ambassadors Group
The Honorable Bethel Nnaemeka Amadi, President, Pan-African Parliament
Amadou Mahtar Ba, Co-founder and Chair, AllAfrica.com
Seth Berkley, Chief Executive Officer, GAVI Alliance
Nancy Birdsall, President, Center for Global Development
Erik Charas, Founder and Managing Director, Charas LDA
Tom Daschle, Former Majority Leader, Unites States Senate
Michael Elliott, President and Chief Executive Officer, The ONE Campaign
Jo Ann Emerson, Chief Executive Officer, National Rural Electric Cooperative Association
Dr. Paul E. Farmer, Co-Founder, Partners in Health
Dr. Helene Gayle, President and Chief Executive Officer, CARE USA
John Githongo, Co-founder, Inuka Ni Sisi Kenya Ltd
The Rev. Mitchell C. Hescox, President/C.E.O., The Evangelical Environmental Network
Richard Horton, BSc MB FRCP FMedSci, Editor, The Lancet
Mike Huckabee, Former Governor, State of Arkansas
General James L. Jones, USMC (Ret.), President, Jones Group International
Julian B. Kiganda, President, African Diaspora for Change
Cathy Leslie, Executive Director, Engineers Without Borders USA
Former Senator Richard Lugar, President, The Lugar Center
Charles Lyons, President and Chief Executive Officer, Elizabeth Glaser Pediatric AIDS Foundation
Darius Mans, President, Africare
Carolyn Miles, President and Chief Executive Officer, Save the Children US
Ory Okolloh, Director of Africa Programs, Omidyar
Arunma Oteh, Director General, Security and Exchange Commission in Nigeria
Lowell (Rusty) Pritchard, Ph.D., President, Flourish/Creation Care Inc.
Jim Presswood, Executive Director, Earth Stewardship Alliance
Rakesh Rajani, Head, Twaweza
Mandla Sibeko, Chief Executive Officer, Icon South Africa
The United Nations Foundation
Evans Wadongo, Founder and Executive Director, Sustainable Development for All—Kenya
World Vision
Kandeh Kolleh Yumkella, Co-Chair, UN High-Level Group on Sustainable Energy for All

Senator COONS. Thank you very much, Mr. Hart.

Mr. Hinks.

STATEMENT OF PAUL HINKS, CHIEF EXECUTIVE OFFICER, SYMBION POWER, WASHINGTON, DC

Mr. HINKS. Chairman Coons, Ranking Member Flake, and distinguished members of the subcommittee, thank you for the opportunity to appear here today.

Large swathes of Africa have no power. Without electric lights, children do homework under paraffin lamps, which are very dangerous. Without electric pumps, villagers have no water and women must walk miles, buckets of water on their heads, babies on their backs. They cannot refrigerate food. They cook on wood or charcoal stoves. The indoor pollution causes large numbers of premature deaths, mostly women and children.

I have seen how electricity transforms a village. Within months, the villagers are using milling machines to grind maize into flour. Go back to that village 5 years later. The place is thriving.

The Power Africa Initiative deserves full bipartisan support. It will be a long-term game-changer for the people of Africa. Here in the United States, jobs will be created and new technologies and products will be deployed in Africa. It is a win-win partnership.

Now a little bit about myself. Since 1980, I have worked on electrification projects in 16 African countries. I am the founder and CEO of Symbion Power, a Washington-based independent power producer and electricity infrastructure engineering contractor. We own three thermal power plants in Tanzania, and as Tony described earlier, we are a partner in a consortium that owns a power plant in Delta State, Nigeria. We are developing power plants in Kenya and Ghana, as well as a new facility in Tanzania in partnership with the government-owned utility TANESCO.

I am also the chairman of the Corporate Council on Africa, which is the largest private sector organization in the United States promoting trade and investment in Africa. CCA member firms represent 85 percent of all United States investment in Africa.

African governments are used to getting loans and grants from development finance institutions such as the World Bank to build power facilities. The Power Africa Initiative is a new model. No pots of money are being distributed as happens with the other agencies. Rather, the private sector is collaborating with the public sector to invest in electricity infrastructure with the United States providing whole-of-government support to the host governments, as well as to the private sector investors.

USAID has made a great start by putting experienced teams in place in the six Power Africa countries, Liberia, Tanzania, Kenya, Ethiopia, Ghana, and Nigeria. Those teams already have facilitated what might be the first-ever power development agreement between the Ethiopian Government and a private sector company, as well as an agreement between the Kenyan Government and a United States generator manufacturer.

I have always believed, however, that it will be more than a year before we see real progress, real new megawatts coming on stream. This new model is not something that everybody is used to working in.

The focus in 2014 should be on addressing some of the significant challenges facing the initiative in order to pave the way for future private sector investment.

One challenge is the reluctance by some in Africa, some politicians, who fear that the private sector power generators will levy higher costs to increase profits. Certainly tariffs must be cost-reflective. Electricity cannot be sold for less than it costs to produce or to buy it. But Power Africa must get across the message that privatization will create efficiencies. Private sector providers can bring to bear their experience and advances in technology to lower production costs and tariffs.

Another serious challenge to the success of power investments in Africa is the creditworthiness or, frankly, lack thereof of some of the off-takers, the government-owned utilities that produce the electricity and distribute it to consumers. If utilities do not pay producers promptly, the producers will, in turn, default on their payments to the very financial institutions such as OPIC, Ex-Im, USTDA, who help fund the investments.

For more than 2 years, my company, Symbion, has been battling in one of the Power Africa countries to be paid fully and to be paid regularly. As of the end of February, we are owed US$70 million for a company that has a turnover of $300 million. This creates problems for a company and it limits our ability to invest in new projects in the same country. Our experience will discourage lenders from funding power projects. It is imperative and urgent that the Power Africa Initiative and U.S. Government agencies address at the highest levels the issue of off-taker creditworthiness across the board to ensure that the economic environment facilitates new investments.

I must add at this point that Nigeria is probably the exception in this case. They have done a fantastic job in their privatization.

Dealing with myriad rules and regulations of multiple bureaucracies in Africa and the United States is one of the biggest challenges. We have not yet seen all of the African host governments cutting through much of the redtape that President Obama spoke about in his speech about the initiative in Tanzania.

And regulatory speed bumps remain in the United States as well. For example, project funding approvals can take 6 months to a year or longer. That is not bad. Sometimes it takes up to 2 years. U.S. agencies should expedite the processes and ensure that they have enough staff to deal quickly with project evaluations.

Finally, Congress' role is absolutely essential to the success of Power Africa. The Electrify Africa Act, championed by Representatives Ed Royce and Karen Bass, along with the Power Africa Initiative will literally light up the lives of hundreds of millions of people in Africa. I hope that this subcommittee and Congress as a whole will agree that the electrification of Africa is a critical goal and that the Power Africa Initiative is a very important step on that way.

Thank you.

[The prepared statement of Mr. Hinks follows:]

PREPARED STATEMENT OF PAUL HINKS

Chairman Coons, Ranking Member Flake, and distinguished members of the subcommittee, thank you for the opportunity to appear before you today to discuss the Power Africa Initiative. I hope I can provide the subcommittee some useful insights into this important program.

INTRODUCTION

By way of introduction, I will provide some brief comments about the Power Africa Initiative and describe a bit of my background, including my experiences with electrification projects in Africa.

When we talk about the lack of access to electricity in sub-Saharan Africa, the hard reality of what it means to the African people often goes over our heads. In some countries, large swathes of the rural population have never had power and, quite frankly, they do not believe they will ever get it.

Without electricity, they have no lights, and their children must do their homework under dangerous paraffin lamps. Using a computer for schoolwork or anything else is impossible, and while there has been an African cell phone revolution, many still have to travel a long way to find someone who has a communal charger.

They cannot get water in their villages because they don't have electric pumps to transport it. Instead, the women—not the men—must walk for miles and miles, carry plastic paint buckets of water on their heads with babies strapped to their backs.. They cannot refrigerate or freeze food, and they cook on biomass-burning stoves, the fuel for which—wood, dung, and charcoal—has to be manually collected—again by women, and by children—causing deforestation, indoor air pollution, and taking children from school. The World Health Organization estimates that those biomass—burning stoves cause two million premature deaths from pneumonia and other illnesses every year worldwide. Most of the victims are women and children. See World Health Organization, Fact Sheet No. 292, Indoor Air Pollution and Health (September 2011), found at http://www.who.int/mediacentre/factsheets/fs292/en/ (last visited March 24, 2014).

No electricity means no development. Over the last three decades I have seen what happens when a village gets electricity for the first time. Within months the villagers start to use milling machines to grind maize into flour and new industry is born. When you return to that same village 5 years later it is thriving, and life has changed forever for its inhabitants.

I was in Africa when the Power Africa Initiative was launched, and I can tell you that it has given hope to hundreds of millions of people. These are rural people with simple lives, and when they hear that the United States is going to help them they believe it. Recently, I was in a village in rural Tanzania for a project inauguration with the Millennium Challenge Corporation, a U.S. Government agency that has electrified hundreds of villages in Tanzania in the past 3 years. The subcommittee would have been touched to see thousands of smiling men, women, and children all waving the U.S. and Tanzania flags. It is nice that we are appreciated in Africa.

This Initiative deserves full bipartisan support. It will be a long-term game changer for the people of Africa, and it is an area where U.S. expertise, U.S. technology, U.S. experience, and U.S.-manufactured products are highly desirable and greatly valued. Many jobs will be created in America, and new U.S. technologies will be deployed. It is a win-win partnership.

MY BACKGROUND

I am the founder and Chief Executive Officer of Symbion Power, a Washington, DC-based Independent Power Producer and electricity infrastructure engineering contractor that has invested in the energy sector in Africa. We own three thermal power plants in Tanzania which generate 217 total megawatts ("MW") of power, and we are a partner in a consortium that owns a 972 MW power plant in Delta State, Nigeria. We also are in the final stages of negotiations for the right to build, own, and operate a geothermal power plant in Kenya, and we are developing a new 450 MW gas facility in Ghana. In addition, we are developing a new 600 MW power facility in southern Tanzania as a public-private partnership with the government-owned power utility TANESCO.

I was trained by the U.K.'s state-owned utility which, at that time, was called the Central Electricity Generating Board. I first went to work in Africa as a young man in 1980 when I worked for the electricity utility of Zimbabwe. After that I worked in Tanzania building electricity infrastructure projects. I lived in Africa, working in the electricity sector, for 10 years, and when I returned to London I continued to work on electrification projects in Africa. At the last count, I have worked on projects in 16 African countries, many of which were facing economic ruin at the time.

From 2003 until 2010 I was heavily involved with the U.S. reconstruction efforts in Iraq and Afghanistan. Working hand in hand with the U.S. military and with the U.S. Government, Symbion Power undertook some of the most difficult and dangerous electrification projects in Iraq, including the 400 kilovolt ("kV") transmission line from Baiji through Haiditha to Al Qaim at the Syrian border. We also built substations in Fallujah, Ramadi, and Sadr City. We were the only U.S. company that worked in those areas between 2005 and 2008 at the height of the insurgency.

In addition to my position at Symbion Power, I have another role here in Washington: I am the Chairman of the Corporate Council on Africa (''CCA''). The CCA is the largest private sector organization in the United States promoting trade and investment in Africa. Some of America's largest corporations are members of the CCA, and CCA member firms represent 85 percent of all U.S. investment in Africa.

WHAT IS POWER AFRICA ALL ABOUT?

As the Chairman of CCA, and as someone with extensive experience in the African power sector, I have been privileged to have been consulted as a representative of the private sector during the development of the Power Africa Initiative. The White House, the State Department, the Department of Commerce, the Department of Energy, USAID and various other government agencies have sought my input from the outset, and I am pleased to say that they have always welcomed, and have carefully considered, my views, which are representative of those of private sector firms who have an interest in power investments and contracting work in Africa.

Dealing with the myriad rules and regulations of multiple bureaucracies in Africa and in the United States is one of the biggest challenges for private sector firms who want to invest in the electricity sector. In his first major speech about the Power Africa Initiative in Dar es Salaam, President Obama, speaking to President Kikwete of Tanzania, emphasized the need to cut through this ''redtape'':

> Now, in order for this to work, then we all have to feel a sense of urgency. One of the things, Mr. President, that I learned around the business roundtable is if we are going to electrify Africa, we've got to do it with more speed. We can't have projects that take, 7, 8, 9 years to be approved and to get online. If we're going to make this happen, we've got to cut through the redtape, and that can only happen with leadership like the leadership that President Kikwete has shown.

Remarks by President Obama at Symbion Ubungo Power Plant, July 2, 2013, (''Pres. Obama Remarks'') found at http://www.whitehouse.gov/the-press-office/2013/07/02/remarks-president-obama-ubungo-symbion-power-plant (last visited March 23, 2014).

Achieving President Obama's stated aim of ''doubling access to electricity,'' starting with ''bring[ing] electricity to 20 million new homes and businesses'' (id.) is not going to be easy, but it is possible if the stakeholders can find a new way of working together. The Power Africa Initiative is that new way of working together, with the U.S. Government providing a ''whole-of-government approach'' to host nations and to the private sector. But these three partners are pretty strange bedfellows.

In Africa, the host governments and the civil servants in ministries are accustomed to a steady flow of development loans and grants from the World Bank, the African Development Bank, and other Development Finance Institutions (''DFIs''), which the governments use to build power-generating facilities. Power Africa is a different model. There are no large pots of money being distributed to the host governments. Rather, the private sector is being asked to step up and invest in electricity infrastructure in Africa, while in parallel USG agencies such as USAID and MCC seek to improve the policy environment and create an enabling environment for U.S. private sector investment in Africa. It will take time for the host governments to become familiar with this new model and to working with the private sector.

Indeed, private sector independent power facilities are still quite rare in Africa. The exception is Nigeria, which has embarked on an aggressive power privatization program in the past 2 years. Privatization is not without controversy; some African politicians and government officials contend that electricity should remain a public sector service provided by the State, citing concerns that because the private sector is required to make a profit there will be pressure to increase retail tariffs, with no consideration for the spending power of their people.

EARLY SUCCESSES

USAID has made a great start on the Power Africa Initiative by putting teams into place in the six Power Africa countries: Liberia, Tanzania, Kenya, Ethiopia, Ghana, and Nigeria. These teams, who collaborate with other U.S. Government agencies, are coordinated out of the Embassy in Nairobi. From what I have seen, they are comprised of experienced, knowledgeable people who can be of great help to the various African governments, their energy ministries, and the respective power utilities. But whilst there are huge power deficits in each of these countries, we don't yet see the sense of ''urgency'' on the part of the host governments that President Obama emphasized is necessary to achieve Power Africa's goals.

Nonetheless, in East Africa, the Power Africa team at USAID has achieved a significant milestone by helping the Ethiopian Government and a project developer execute what might be the first-ever power development agreement with a private sector company in that country. The developer, a New York-based investment firm, has projected that this renewable energy geothermal power plant eventually will deliver 1,000 MW of power to the East African grid. And in Kenya, the Power Africa team has assisted a U.S. generator manufacturer who is one of the members at CCA, to execute an agreement with the Kenya Government.

ADJUSTING TO THE NEW WAY OF WORKING WILL TAKE TIME

These are early victories that represent real progress for the Power Africa Initiative. But I have always believed that it will take over a year before we see tangible results in the form of new megawatts—that is, megawatts that were not previously under development—coming on-stream in Africa. Power Africa is ground-breaking, and it will take time for the three new bedfellows—the U.S. Government, African host nations, and the private sector—to adjust to working together in a new way. The focus in 2014 should be on addressing some of the significant challenges facing the Power Africa Initiative, in order to pave the way for more private-sector investment in the future.

I have already mentioned one of those challenges: the fear that private sector power generators will levy higher costs to increase profits. Addressing this concern is already on the Power Africa agenda: one of the clear messages of Power Africa, the DFIs and the private sector is that tariffs must be cost-reflective—electricity cannot be sold for less than it costs to produce. But private sector providers can bring to bear their experience and advances in technology to ensure that power production costs, and therefore tariffs, are kept as low as possible. Through Power Africa, the United States must work at political and administrative levels on the continent to better explain the role of the private sector and the benefits that can be achieved in terms of efficiency if privatization programs are properly implemented.

SECURITY OF PAYMENT AND CREDITWORTHINESS IS A CRITICAL ISSUE

Another serious challenge to the success of power investments in Africa is the creditworthiness, or lack thereof, of the ''off-takers'' which are usually the government-owned utilities that purchase the electricity from the power producers and distribute it to the consumers. In most instances, the state-owned utility cannot demonstrate a sufficient level of assurance that it will be in a position to pay the private sector producers or that it will pay promptly and in accordance with the terms of the contract. In practice, if the producers are not paid, they will in turn default on their payments to banks and other financial institutions who help fund the investments that have very little tolerance for nonpayment.

For more than 2 years, my company, Symbion Power, has been battling in one of the Power Africa countries to get paid fully and regularly, to the point where, as of February, 2014, we are owed $70 million USD. The debt will be even greater at the end of March when more invoices are submitted. This level of debt is simply unsustainable for a company of our size. Whilst we have confidence that the host government eventually will pay us, the cash-flow problems that the situation has created cause considerable disruption to our operations.

Our experience will have a negative effect on lenders' willingness to fund power projects in that country, and if lenders will not fund large-scale—or even small-scale—private sector development, the aims of Power Africa in that country will not be met. It is therefore imperative and urgent that the Power Africa Initiative and all agencies of the U.S. Government address at the highest levels the issue of off-taker creditworthiness so that the economic environment facilitates new investments. Not being paid on time or at all is at the top of the fear list for the private sector.

URGENCY AND SPEED

To achieve the speed of development that the President has emphasized is necessary to meet the ever-growing need for electricity in Africa, the various U.S. Government agencies involved in the Power Africa Initiative should examine how they can expedite their processes. The normal lead times for project funding approvals can be in the range of 6 months to 1 year, but it is often much longer. These agencies are bound by rules and regulations that do not necessarily foster alacrity, and if some dispensations are made we will see faster results and more power, quickly, in Africa.

Some in the private sector have also raised the question whether the U.S. agencies will have sufficient human resources to deal with a large influx of project evaluations. This issue obviously must be addressed by the agencies themselves; I note only that the private sector is concerned that it may not get the attention and speed needed when projects are submitted for consideration and funding approval.

Finally, I want to emphasize that Congress's role is absolutely essential to the success of Power Africa. The Electrify Africa Act—which is being championed by Representative Ed Royce, chairman of the House Committee on Foreign Affairs, and by Representative Karen Bass, ranking member of the Subcommittee on Africa—coupled with the Power Africa Initiative itself, will literally light up the lives of those hundreds of millions of people in Africa. Those of us who spend our time working in the power sector on the African Continent do so because we know that reliable power is essential to the economic development of Africa and because we know just how much it will improve the lives of the African people. I hope that this subcommittee and Congress as a whole will agree that the electrification of Africa is an important goal, and that the Power Africa Initiative is an important step in achieving that goal.

Senator COONS. Thank you very much, Mr. Hinks.

I would like to thank our entire panel.

Our 12 o'clock vote is going to be called any moment now. So if I might, I am going to suggest a series of questions. We will stay and listen to the answers as long as we can, and then, frankly, if you will forgive us, we are going to depart to go cast our votes on a foreign relations related matter.

First, several of you have referenced the importance of a whole-of-government approach, Mr. Hinks in particular. One concern we share is that there are 12 different agencies to which different potential partners, private sector and coordinating public sector agencies, that have to work together. How can we do a better job of reducing duplication, overlap, and streamlining the review and approval process that is currently being led through USAID? Mr. Renigar, Mr. Hinks. First.

Second, if I might, to Mr. Hart, there is some concern about overemphasis on large-scale centralized power, the high-low that Mr. Renigar referred to. It is great that GE has partnered with ADF on a significant sort of off-grid and renewable demonstration project, but the scale of centralized power versus the distributed in this overall initiative is significantly, as it were, high-low. Do we need to be doing more, Mr. Hart, in order to ensure that the most remote, most rural, most distant from access to grid systems and centralized power are in fact served and our development goals are in fact met?

Mr. Elumelu, what are the biggest barriers to ensuring a strong African private sector partnership? This is a great start. Thank you for your partnership, but what are the remaining largest barriers?

If we might, in turn with those three questions, and we will do our best to listen. Thank you to the entire panel.

Mr. HINKS. On the question of the interagency, intergovernment approach, to be quite honest, we have seen an exceptional collaboration taking place between the various Government agencies. We have been working with USAID, with OPIC, with Ex-Im, all of them. And really, the Power Africa Working Group or the Power Africa group in Kenya is working across all those agencies and coordinating things. And we are not seeing, I would say, duplication.

We are seeing cooperation between them. So my words for the interagency part of this are only good of what we have seen so far.

The issue of the delays I talked about is that if we are going to have urgency, which is the language that President Obama used, we have to get funding urgently. And if funding is going to take 1 year or 18 months, 2 years, we are not going to achieve anything fast. So the way I see it is there are things that could be done within the agencies to speed up the process of project evaluation, due diligence, getting congressional approvals, et cetera, et cetera. I believe that can be done.

Senator COONS. Thank you, Mr. Hinks.

Speaking of urgency, our vote has been called.

Mr. Hart, anything on high-low and distributed power and access for rural?

Mr. HART. Very, very briefly, yes. The initiative has to focus on the hardest to reach or it simply will not happen. Projects will go to the lowest hanging fruit, the most efficient, easiest to reach. So that has to be a priority of the initiative, both Power Africa and the legislation.

Let me also say that it is not also sufficient just to do solar lanterns in remote villages. Off-grid, mini-grid, renewable units that harness natural gas locally, all of these things need to be focused on in order to get the poorest and most needy the electricity they deserve.

Senator COONS. I will note that today Africa as a continent has the highest percentage of renewable power generation, as Mr. Elumelu pointed out in his testimony. Our hope is to sustain that by a truly all-of-the-above strategy which we will turn to when we look at legislation.

Mr. Elumelu, you get to have the last word. What are the remaining major barriers to effective partnership——

Mr. ELUMELU. I think first would be for this Electrify Africa Act to be passed, to play a key role in helping to open up the continent as relates to the core objective of increasing access to electricity. So that is what we want.

Two is policy reforms. As we heard from Paul, in some African countries, they are setting policy inhibitions that actually are affecting the realization of this wonderful initiative of improving access to electricity. My solution on that would be that the U.S. Government should please have to encourage African political leaders and institutions to embark on reforms that will help to improve access to electricity.

The third point is getting some form of guarantee that can support the private sector investment in this.

Thank you so much.

Senator COONS. Thank you very much.

I will invite a closing comment from Senator Flake, and then we will keep the record open until close of business on Thursday, April 3, for any additional questions from members of the subcommittee who were unable to attend today.

Senator Flake.

Senator FLAKE. Thank you.

And we apologize for our schedule here. But this was very thoughtful testimony, very useful, enjoyed reading it, and we will look forward to studying it in the future.

Mr. Elumelu, thank you again for traveling so far, and thank you for, in both your written and oral testimony, talking about the carbon footprint, if you will, for every African and how much lower it is, .3 tons per person, compared to the United States, as much as 15 tons per person. And that speaks to me of the need to make sure that the goal to power Africa and to bring power is not subverted for other agendas. So it was very important testimony.

All of you, thank you for being here.

Senator COONS. Thank you, Senator Flake.

I would like to thank all the members of our second panel and our first panel for some very insightful and broad testimony. I look forward to working together as we move to the consideration of the Power Africa bill going forward. Thank you very much.

[Whereupon, at 12:07 p.m., the hearing was adjourned.]

ADDITIONAL MATERIAL SUBMITTED FOR THE RECORD

WRITTEN STATEMENT FROM DANIEL W. YOHANNES, CHIEF EXECUTIVE OFFICER, MILLENNIUM CHALLENGE CORPORATION

Chairman Coons, Ranking Member Flake, and members of the Subcommittee on African Affairs, the Millennium Challenge Corporation (MCC) appreciates this opportunity to describe our critical contributions to the USG Power Africa initiative, and commends you for convening this hearing to draw attention to this ambitious and very worthy initiative. We particularly appreciate the opportunity to outline the significant contributions that MCC has made and will make toward the goal of bringing electricity to Africa.

Before there was a Power Africa initiative, MCC was funding power in Africa. In a compact with Tanzania signed in 2008, MCC funded approximately $200 million in power sector investments. As a requirement of this compact, the Government of Tanzania passed the first comprehensive revision to an electricity law dating back to 1931, which was far too dated to address current market needs. As a result of MCC's engagement with the government through the compact, Tanzanian regulators approved new, more cost-reflective tariffs, a key step toward bringing in private sector investment. MCC is currently working with the Government of Tanzania to develop a new compact that would include an even more comprehensive program of sector reforms that are intended to establish a more efficient, well-managed and creditworthy power utility that will operate in a competitive market place.

Since our inception 10 years ago, MCC has funded programs across a wide variety of sectors and disciplines of international development. The common thread across MCC's commitments—whether a port in Benin, land tenure programs in Burkina Faso, education in Namibia, or a 100 MW submarine cable between Zanzibar and mainland Tanzania—is that economic analysis and country commitment underpin sector and project choices. Increasingly, African countries are discovering that one of their major constraints to economic growth is their lack of reliable power, and they are committing to tackling this constraint.

As partner countries in Africa identify energy poverty and insecurity as binding constraints to economic growth, they are developing their compacts funded by MCC to address this pressing challenge. Increasingly, MCC compacts in Africa are being designed to increase and improve access to reliable and affordable electricity. This means investing in energy infrastructure, policy and regulatory reforms and institutional capacity-building in the power sector.

Of the six Power Africa countries, three are current MCC partners: Ghana, Liberia, and Tanzania. MCC is working with these governments to identify potential projects which will seek to address the nations' inadequate and unreliable power supply. These countries have set ambitious goals in electric power generation and are taking the steps to reform the utility and energy sectors to pave the way for investment and growth. Through the Power Africa initiative MCC will work with host governments to help increase technical skills and accelerate energy sector regulatory, market structure and enabling environment reforms that are critical to the sustainability of the sector and projects.

In addition to the $200 million already invested in Tanzania, MCC plans to invest up to $1 billion in Ghana, Tanzania, and Liberia's power sectors. Although Africa needs approximately $40 billion annually to meet its power needs, only about a third of the investment requirements are currently being met. MCC will help fill the gap through investments in the sector. A reformed and competitive power market, which MCC will also support, should attract private sector investment to fill this gap.

In Ghana, two main reasons for low levels of private capital in the power sector are the lack of creditworthy off-takers and non-cost-reflective tariffs. To that end, the Public Utilities Regulatory Commission recently announced a 79 percent increase in tariffs. This important step toward cost recovery accompanies a commitment by the government to use an automatic adjustment mechanism to keep the rates reflective of evolving costs. The government has also committed to bring similar order to the pricing and supply of gas—a critical fuel for power generation.

MCC is working with the Government of Ghana to evaluate private sector participation to help the utility become a creditworthy entity. MCC has also proven the importance of integrating private sector input in program design early on in Ghana's compact development process. In fact, MCC's work has already scored a significant success before the compact has even been signed; General Electric credited MCC's compact and associated reforms with being a major factor in its plans to build a 1,000 megawatt power park and associated infrastructure in Ghana—a $1.5 billion financial commitment.

Working with other agencies in the Power Africa initiative, MCC will maximize its power sector investments. USAID technical assistance and EX–IM and OPIC products can help unlock commercial debt and equity capital, while the use of USTDA studies can reduce the early stage risk for companies.

MCC's work on energy extends to Malawi, which is not currently a Power Africa country. MCC's $350 million compact in Malawi is focused on the turnaround of the power utility and related sector reforms. The government is taking steps to establish a market-friendly power sector, and the results have been encouraging. A number of key sector reforms have been implemented, the balance sheet of the utility has been cleaned up and the government has agreed to implement a restructuring program to prepare for a competitive power market which includes various options for increasing private sector involvement in the power sector.

In countries that meet MCC's good governance standards, MCC will work in partnership with country governments to uncover opportunities for economic growth, and when lack of energy is a constraint to economic growth, MCC has the proven ability to fund infrastructure, leverage private sector financing and investment, and commit to improving energy sector policies and institutions. MCC is proud to be part of the USG-wide partnership initiative that is Power Africa.

Letter From 13 Organizations to Senators Christopher A. Coons and Jeff Flake Concerning the Power Africa Initiative

25 March 2014.

Hon. Chris Coons, *Chairman,*
Hon. Jeff Flake, *Ranking Member,*
Subcommittee on African Affairs,
Committee on Foreign Affairs,
Washington, DC.

Dear Chairman Coons and Ranking Member Flake: Our organizations have followed with interest the Power Africa Initiative and the progress of the Electrify Africa Act of 2014 in the House and still to be introduced Senate bill. We believe there is a great opportunity for development and environmental organizations to work together with Congress and key private sector allies to bring inclusive, environmentally and socially sustainable energy to the people of sub-Saharan Africa. In advance of the March 27 subcommittee hearing on the Power Africa Initiative, we want to share with you key principles we see as priorities for initiatives that aim to address electricity access in Africa.

★ *ACCESS:* We believe that one of the greatest potential strengths of the Power Africa Initiative and the Electrify Africa Act is to promote electricity access that is truly inclusive as a tool for development. Our organizations feel very strongly that an initiative focused on energy access must emphasize providing energy to populations currently without access and with intermittent access, focusing on households and services—such as health care and education—in poor, rural, and marginalized communities. Achieving this will require an emphasis on sustainable off-grid and mini-grid energy production and distribution projects.

★ *RENEWABLES:* In expanding electricity access, development goals are best served and effectively implemented when clean, renewable energy sources, including off-grid and mini-grid solutions, are prioritized, fully accounting for the environmental and social externalities of fossil fuel projects; and when energy efficiency and demand-side management are a central part of electricity expansion strategies. Also, our organizations feel strongly that the Power Africa Initiative and Electrify Africa Act should not instigate any weakening of the greenhouse gas emissions cap at the Overseas Private Investment Corporation, a policy which has made OPIC a development investment leader in renewables projects that increase energy access.

★ *GOVERNANCE:* We believe that the promotion of electricity access should be accompanied by support for inclusive, transparent, and accountable processes for electricity production and distribution planning, implementation, and management. These efforts should ensure compliance with international best practice fiduciary standards and social and environmental safeguards. In cases of potentially significant environmental and social impacts, communities must have the right to free, prior and informed consent to projects.

We welcome an opportunity to meet with you to discuss further details and how we could be of assistance in shaping the Senate legislation to authorize and expand the Administration's Power Africa Initiative.

Sincerely,

Center for Biological Diversity; Center for International Environmental Law; Foreign Policy in Focus; Friends of the Earth; Greenpeace; Institute for Policy Studies Climate Policy Program; International Rivers; Natural Resources Defense Council; Oil Change International; Oxfam America; Pacific Environment; United Methodist Church General Board of Church and Society; Vasudha Foundation USA.

Written Statement From Shari Berenbach, President/CEO, United States African Development Foundation

Chairman Coons, Ranking Member Flake, and members of the Subcommittee on African Affairs, thank you for the opportunity to provide written testimony on President Obama's Power Africa Initiative. We would like to share with you the experience of the U.S. African Development Foundation (USADF) in Africa's renewable energy sector, particularly the Power Africa Off-Grid Energy Challenge we are undertaking in partnership with GE Africa.

ABOUT USADF

Founded by an Act of Congress in 1980, the U.S. African Development Foundation (USADF) provides direct development assistance at the grassroots level to support African-designed and -driven solutions to economic challenges. USADF operates as a public corporation in the United States Government (USG) to support the economic development of marginalized and underserved populations. USADF directly funds African cooperatives, small- and medium-sized enterprises (SMEs), community-based organizations, and African technical service organizations. Together, they work to increase economic activities, improve livelihoods, and establish sustainable businesses.

USADF, as the sole USG agency focused exclusively on Africa, has an ever-increasing role to play in the continent. USADF operates in 18 countries in Africa, with an emphasis on the Sahel and the Horn of Africa, where we are supporting marginalized communities to foster resilience and new economic opportunities, critical for restoring peace, stability, and economic independence.

NEED FOR OFF-GRID RENEWABLE ENERGY

The marginalized communities in need of economic opportunities supported by USADF are vastly underserved by the conventional electrical grid currently in Africa. Not only does the grid not reach these communities today, it is unlikely to do so for the foreseeable future. In fact, a number of sources contend that even in the long-run, these rural communities will be best served by a new generation of technology that is making off-grid solutions both reliable and cost-effective. Just as cell phones revolutionized the delivery of telecommunication services to remote regions, leapfrogging the need for costly land-line installations, we anticipate a new generation of off-gird solutions that will be launched and implemented by creative SMEs to develop and operate mini-grid and off-grid approaches to meet the energy needs of Africa's rural poor.

No doubt, you have already received substantial testimony that addresses the need and opportunity for lighting-up Africa across much of the continent. In the six Power Africa countries alone, over 230 million people live without access to electricity. In east Africa, four out of five people live without access to power. In a country such as Liberia, only one out of twenty people have access to power.

USADF witnesses on a regular basis how this lack of power curbs economic prospects. Farmers could benefit from electricity to power local processing of agricultural products. Enterprises could work longer hours, produce could be refrigerated and more food could make it to market—all contributing toward the goals of increased productivity, food security and improved household incomes.

On a more human level, data shows that access to electricity can significantly benefit rural households. Children are able to study when light is available in the evening. Cleaner cooking technologies benefit women and children, as well as the environment. Clinics with access to electricity will be able to maintain needed vaccines and offer a lighted theater for childbirth and other urgent medical care. Schools with electricity can operate longer hours and serve more needs of the communities. Lighting matters!

GE—USADF POWER AFRICA OFF-GRID ENERGY CHALLENGE—LAUNCHING NEW BUSINESS MODELS

With such great need for electricity in rural areas, USADF has teamed up with GE Africa to launch the Power Africa Off-Grid Energy Challenge. The goal of this challenge is to support a new generation of business models for the generation and distribution of renewable energy to meet the needs of marginalized, underserved communities in Africa.

By mandate, USADF solely funds 100 percent African owned and managed enterprises—so we have sought out African SMEs, organizations and associations that are developing profitable, sustainable approaches to bringing energy to rural communities. And, as we know, "Angel Investing"—popular in the U.S. for funding new technologies—is virtually nonexistent in Africa. To overcome this gap, the Off-Grid Energy Challenge is providing $100,000 grants to these African companies and organizations to test new prototypes and scale-up delivery of energy to rural communities operating beyond the grid.

The first round of the Challenge was launched last July just days after President Obama announced Power Africa and was limited to entries from Kenya and Nigeria. As we know, there is no shortage of smarts and initiative among entrepreneurs in these countries, so there should be little surprise to the outpouring of interest and enthusiasm for the Challenge. In just a few weeks after the launch, the Challenge received nearly 150 applications—equally split between the two countries—with ideas ranging from solar to bio-gas to wind to hydro and every combination you could possibly imagine. USADF assembled a panel of judges that included not only individuals from USADF and GE Africa, but also experts from the Millennium Challenge Corporation, the World Bank, and the Shell Foundation. In November 2013, in Lagos, GE and USADF announced the first round of grant winners:

- Solar World (E.A.) Ltd. will construct 5 solar-powered water points to provide water and electricity to pastoralists in the semiarid lands in northern Kenya.
- Afrisol Energy Ltd. will utilize biodigesters to produce electricity and biogas for small businesses in Nairobi's urban slums.
- Mibawa Suppliers will expand its delivery of pay-as-you-go lighting and chargers to households in rural parts of western Kenya.
- TransAfrica Gas and Electric will power stand-alone cold storage facilities with solar photovoltaic systems for farmers and fisherman in Jos, northern Nigeria.
- GVE Projects Ltd. will electrify 24 off-grid communities in Nigeria using metered solar photovoltaic microgrid and portable rechargeable battery systems, targeted to customers' demands.
- Afe Babalola University in Nigeria will investigate hydroelectric and solar systems to serve students and faculty, and the neighboring community of 10,000+, who currently rely on diesel generators.

USADF and GE Africa are now gearing up for a second round of the Challenge. This time the effort will expand to business solutions from all six Power Africa countries. Along with support from USADF and GE Africa, USAID has come on-board to add to the total pool of funding needed for grant awards, as well as technical support for the winners once they are awarded. This second round will be launched in

May 2014 and we expect to announce three winners per country, for a total of 18 awards in September 2014.

Experts from across the field have commended this sort of Challenge as it provides essential seed capital to test new business models—that can lead toward profitable, sustainable business solutions to meet the energy needs of Africa's rural and underserved communities.

CONCLUSION: POWERING AFRICA

Power Africa has set out to meet an urgent need—to electrify the millions of businesses, homes, clinics, and schools that lack access to basic energy services. While much of this need will be met with proven technology for conventional energy generation and distribution in the urban centers of Africa, there is an unprecedented opportunity to support new sustainable approaches to meet the energy needs of rural communities beyond the grid. We believe that this extraordinary challenge will be met by a new generation of energy entrepreneurs who will bring innovative solutions and new business approaches to overcome today's energy gap. In so doing, we will be creating economic opportunity for those on the margins and laying the foundation for a brighter future for all of Africa.

Thank you.

LETTER FROM JOHN COEQUYT, DIRECTOR, INTERNATIONAL CLIMATE PROGRAMS, SIERRA CLUB

SIERRA CLUB,
March 27, 2014.

Senator CHRISTOPHER COONS,
Russell Senate Office Building,
Washington, DC.

DEAR SENATOR COONS: Thank you for opportunity to submit testimony for today's hearing on the Power Africa Initiative.

The President's Power Africa initiative has brought much-needed attention to the critical problem of energy poverty in Africa. Across the world, there are still 1.3 billion people living in severe energy poverty today, almost half of whom (587 million) live in sub-Saharan Africa. It has become increasingly clear that the traditional approach to this problem—increasing electricity supply by building large, centralized power plants feeding into a geographically extensive grid—will not be sufficient to address this challenge with appropriate urgency or at an acceptable cost. Grid extension projects often are not an effective approach for reaching the majority of the people in need of energy, who are rural and poor. They often take a long time to bring online, and even when the grid reaches communities the cost of interconnection is often beyond reach. Indeed, perhaps due to the prohibitive cost, the initial round of Power Africa proposals focuses almost exclusively on expanding supply of electricity, with scant attention to delivering it to those who need it through grid extension.

Rather than thinking about energy poverty primarily as a problem of supply and distribution of electricity, it is more useful to frame the challenge as one of expanding access to modern energy services. This approach begins by asking what energy services the poor most need to enhance their development opportunities, and then determining the best way to provide those services. Recent technological and financial innovations have created a wealth of new opportunities to expand access to those critical services for the world's energy poor. Dramatic improvements in solar technologies have reduced the costs of solar home systems considerably. At the same time, game-changing improvements in the efficiency of consumer appliances such as lights, cell phone chargers, fans, and televisions have enabled smaller, cheaper solar systems to deliver more energy services at lower cost. Moreover, social entrepreneurs have developed innovative financial models that enable the poor to avoid paying the prohibitive upfront costs of these systems. Instead, they can now pay over time, which results in monthly charges that are often much less than they are currently paying for vastly inferior kerosene-based energy services or what they would pay to access to the grid.

To capture the benefits of new technologies and financial models and move beyond outdated approaches, Power Africa should strike a balance among grid extension, mini-grid, and off-grid solutions. Of these three approaches, we currently see the least emphasis on, and most need for, distributed clean, renewable energy sources that power mini-grids and off-grid solutions. In their "Energy for All" case—the scenario required to provide modern energy for all by 2030—the IEA allocates 64 percent of additional (above the "New Policies Scenario") annual energy investments to mini-grid and isolated off-grid solutions. Yet distributed clean energy is the least supported of the energy access solutions in sub-Saharan Africa.

Off-grid, distributed programs that have been supported with targeted public money are growing rapidly, and have established an impressive record of success. In Bangladesh, companies like Grameen Shakti are deploying 60,000 solar home systems every single month. Already the country has installed over 2 million systems. In sub-Saharan Africa, Lighting Africa estimates the off-grid solar lighting market is growing at a 95 percent compound annual growth rate. Just one of those companies, d.light, has empowered 28.7 million people with solar lighting, including 7 million school-aged children. The development benefits of these installations are enormous: they contribute to the empowerment of women, education of children, effectiveness of health care, and growth of the local economy.

Significantly, these companies make energy affordable for poor consumers today, whether they are connected to the grid or not. Rather than paying large amounts of upfront costs on grid connection or monthly energy bills, customers can pay on a pay-as-you-go basis, using mobile phone-based money transfer platforms. M-KOPA Solar in Kenya, for example, has used a mobile money platform to provide solar power to over 50,000 Kenyan households. They have since secured $20 million in private investment and expect to serve 1 million households by 2018.

These rapid off-grid solutions provide a critical first step onto the energy ladder with basic energy services such as lighting, mobile phone charging, fans, and now, super-efficient televisions. Most importantly, this happens on a time scale that accelerates impact: days and months, not the years and decades they often must wait for centralized power plants and grid extension. Then, as their income, and their country's infrastructure, grows, people can move up the energy ladder to consume more energy services such as refrigeration. Lighting and mobile phone charging are the beginning, not the end of energy access.

While distributed renewables are essential for rural populations, they also fill important needs for other populations. For many urban Africans and the growing middle class, the centralized grid is unreliable and provides just a few hours of power each day. Solar companies have found an important customer base among grid connected populations seeking more reliable power through solar and battery technology. Solar panels on these roofs helps to keep the electricity flowing even when the grid is not working.

Finally, distributed generation can empower the poor in the political sense as well as in the developmental one. Often, the poor have not been afforded access to modern energy services due to governance reasons as much as technological or economic reasons. Decisionmakers may not see expanding affordable access as a priority, and the poor often lack the means to hold them accountable. With the deployment of distributed generation such as solar home systems, access to energy is no longer dependent on political decisions regarding where the grid will be extended, or how much utilities can charge. Smaller project sizes associated with distributed clean energy removes the ability of governing elites to centralize and control resources, and limits opportunities for corruption.

Despite these advantages of off-grid renewables, support from the Power Africa Initiative has been skewed toward large scale power plants, without costly grid extension. Clean energy has received significantly less support. To better balance its approach, the administration should expand its support for off-grid and mini-grid energy access projects. For example, Power Africa should implement a dedicated loan guarantees for distributed renewable energy projects. In many Power Africa countries, banks are hesitant to take on the risks of loans to a new company or to players in an emerging sector. Loan guarantees can therefore stimulate local lending and provide an opportunity for local banks to gain comfort with entrepreneurs in this sector over time, and thus provide desperately needed working capital across the supply chain. With greater access to local resources, solar system providers can scale up their operations and get products and power into people's hands quickly. Expanded finance for these innovative solar entrepreneurs would allow their work to reach an unprecedented scale. Even a fraction of the Power Africa budget devoted to off-grid solutions could help these markets grow at exponential rates similar to mobile phone adoption in the early 2000s.

Distributed solutions need to play a bigger role in this initiative, and in public electrification efforts, than they have. In order to do that the industry needs public support. Over the past several years OPIC has become a key source of support for distributed renewable energy solutions. Important energy access programs like the African Clean Energy Finance (ACEF) Initiative leverage the investment made available by OPIC to support clean energy, including off-grid and mini-grid interventions. This means more dollars for programs on the ground and more people getting energy access. It is essential that OPIC continue to support programs like ACEF.

Many have sought to frame this issue as an environmental or climate imperative. It is not. This is about choosing the right tool for the energy access job. In many cases, distributed clean energy is the preferred option. If we are able to move beyond business as usual we can help catalyze a 21st century transition in Africa. Just as mobile phones have leapfrogged landlines, distributed renewables can leapfrog centralized grids. It's time we unlock the world's most sophisticated technologies for the world's poorest populations. Only that can be truly considered empowerment.

Thank you again for the opportunity to submit comments to this hearing.

Sincerely,

JOHN COEQUYT,
Director,
International Climate Programs.

RESPONSE OF TOM HART TO QUESTION
SUBMITTED BY SENATOR ROBERT MENENDEZ

Question. M–KOPA, a company based in Kenya, sells a home power system composed of a small solar panel, a battery, two ceiling lights, a portable light, a radio, and slots to charge five cell phones simultaneously. The company recently raised over $20 million in private financing, which M–KOPA says will allow it to expand its customer base from 50,000 now, to 1 million by 2018. M–KOPA is clearly an example of an innovative business that is rapidly expanding in order to effectively serve people living off-grid. What can we do to help M–KOPA and similar companies address critical energy access issues in sub-Saharan Africa?

Answer. Thank you, Mr. Chairman. Given the magnitude of the electricity deficit in Africa, ONE supports scaling up investments in innovative off-grid renewable technologies as well as increasing financing for traditional on-grid power solutions. Numerous U.S. Government agencies can assist companies like M–KOPA depending on their ownership structure (i.e., companies that have a U.S. connection or wholly African owned) and financing needs. OPIC, the World Bank, African Development Bank, USAID's Development Credit Authority, the U.S. African Development Foundation, Millennium Challenge Corporation and others are increasing access to finance and technical assistance to companies. We believe African entrepreneurs are a key part of successfully addressing energy poverty. In partnership with African governments and African financial institutions, enactment of legislation to build on the President's Power Africa initiative would be critical to ensuring people living in sub-Saharan Africa have access to the most appropriate technologies to meet their energy needs.

Getting reliable electricity access to the poorest and most underserved areas will require special effort, and we believe the legislation should specifically address this challenge. Picking only the low hanging fruit would leave millions without energy.

RESPONSE OF PAUL HINKS TO QUESTION
SUBMITTED BY SENATOR ROBERT MENENDEZ

Question. You have cited Symbion Power's difficulty in getting the Tanzanian utility TANESCO to pay the $70 million it owes your company. How much of that debt stems from the Emergency Power Contracts you have with TANESCO? Is there an opportunity to reduce the high tariff rates under the Emergency Power Contracts so that TANESCO will be able to repay its debt, but Symbion will still enjoy a sizeable profit?

Answer. Symbion owns and operates three power plants in Tanzania. One, which is in Dar es Salaam, has a net output of 112MW. Symbion charges 4.9 cents per Kwh for this plant. This is a gas-fired power plant and the gas is supposed to be provided to the power plant by the national power utility TANESCO. Unfortunately, 2 years ago, the amount of gas available in Dar es Salaam became limited when TANESCO introduced a new power plant, which they own. Instead of providing gas to the Symbion plant per our contract, they asked us to convert our GE aeroderivative gas turbines to run on Jet A liquid fuel. The turbines are four GE jet engines coupled to generators. The cost of running an aeroderivative gas turbine with Jet A fuel is enormously expensive.

The other two plants are in more rural areas of Tanzania—Dodoma (55 MW) and Arusha (50MW). The charge per Kwh for those two plants is roughly half a cent more than the plant in Dar es Salaam—5.5 cents. Because there is no other source of fuel there, these plants also have to run on liquid fuel which in this case is diesel. Both plants were imported and installed on an emergency fast-track basis in 2011 and 2012. Once again, because of the cost of fuel, it is very expensive to run 105MW far from the place where the fuel is imported. It has to be trucked every day from Dar es Salaam.

The rates Symbion is charging are fair given the cost of operating. The problem for TANESCO is that the fuel we have to use is expensive Jet A and diesel. Symbion were contracted to buy the fuel and then get reimbursed at cost (with no profit margin on top of it) by TANESCO but this never happens in a timely manner so in fact we have been financing the fuel—and therefore the electricity for the people of Tanzania—for 2 years now.

Symbion is not making excessive profits from its power plants in Tanzania, and we have to carry huge interest costs to support the debt from TANESCO which seriously erodes any profit that we make. The costs of operating and maintaining the equipment in Tanzania—and especially in rural areas—is also expensive. The real problem is not Symbion's costs but that there is insufficient gas in Dar es Salaam and that the two plants in Dodoma and Arusha utilize diesel causing high costs.

Because of our commitment to the Tanzania Government and the people of Tanzania, we have never taken any action that would result in an interruption of power to the country. We have a very good relationship with TANESCO and the GOT. At certain times of the year when the hydroelectric plants do not run because of drought conditions, Symbion represents 30 percent of the total available capacity which means that we are a very critical supplier.

The large debt that has accumulated could be paid if the GOT injected funds into TANESCO, but it seems they are reluctant to do that. The level of the debt is unsustainable for a company of our size and it is limiting Symbion's operations and other new Power Africa equity investments because of the resultant constant cash-flow problems. We are developing new investments in Tanzania that will need cash as well as in Nigeria, Ghana and Kenya.

Symbion has given outstanding support to the Tanzania Government. Our investments are coupled with social programs that include a training school for overhead power linemen in Morogoro where we have trained hundreds of workers to U.S. standards, a school for the underprivileged in Morogoro, an HIV/AIDS program called "Transmit Electricity Not Aids," a Sports Park in central Dar es Salaam, and a new development for a soccer academy which is a collaboration with Sunderland Football Club, an English Premier League Team. We have set a new standard in the level of community programs we have embarked on and we believe we have been an excellent flag bearer for the United States of America.

Response of Del Renigar to Question Submitted by Senator Robert Menendez

Question. In your testimony, you stated that in order to allow natural gas to be used for power in sub-Saharan Africa, "we need to be looking at subsidies. . . ." This is not the first time we have heard about GE advising African governments to subsidize natural gas.

- Does GE advise governments to do this? If so, is this suitable advice, considering that natural gas subsidies are contrary to U.S. policy, can distort electricity markets, can lead to enormous debts for utilities and governments, as well as inefficient use of natural gas, and, at least in the case of Ukraine, can help spark international crises?

Answer. On behalf of GE, thank you for the opportunity to clarify any misunderstanding of the Company's position on natural gas pricing and allocation policies.

As noted in the Power Africa Reforms section of the written testimony, the inability to take full advantage of Africa's vast natural gas reserves is a serious issue on the continent. GE's position is that to bridge this gap, to develop African economies, and to raise quality of life for their people, governments in the region must create a regulatory framework that brings natural gas on shore and successfully links it to power generation.

An effective enabling policy requires a sensible approach to natural gas pricing and allocation. The status quo includes fuel subsidies in many countries, which may distort the market. When my oral statement noted that these subsidies should be "looked at," it was in reference to GE's position that the subsidies and their disruptions should be reconsidered so that a more market-based system can emerge to enable natural gas to assume a competitive role among other, currently subsidized fuels. To be clear, we do not, and have not, and have no intention of advocating for subsidies for natural gas in Africa or elsewhere. Ultimately, energy security and prosperity in Africa and elsewhere will depend on a broad and diverse range of energy sources, and efficient and effective policies to ensure their development and management.

RESPONSES OF HON. MIMI ALEMAYEHOU TO QUESTIONS SUBMITTED BY SENATOR ROBERT MENENDEZ

Question. Given OPIC's commitment to renewable energy, and the fact that OPIC's portfolio is well under the carbon cap it has been operating under, has the carbon cap truly hindered OPIC's operations?

Answer. OPIC's $1.5 billion commitment to Power Africa was premised in part on careful calculations of the Green House Gas (GHG) emissions that would be allowable under the reduction targets then in force. These GHG emissions should be sufficient to accommodate approximately 800 MW of thermal power production, in addition to the existing robust pipeline of renewable energy projects.

The Electrify Africa bill that has been approved by the House of Representatives contains more ambitious power generation and access goals than the Power Africa initiative. To achieve the Electrify Africa goals, OPIC would need the flexibility to finance a broader mix of energy resources. But it bears noting that OPIC, an inherently market-driven agency, has not financed a coal-fired power plant since 1996. This was more than a decade before the focus on renewable energy and the creation of the GHG emissions reduction plan.

OPIC anticipates that the suspension of its GHG emissions reduction goals in IDA-eligible countries for FY14, as mandated by the FY14 Omnibus Appropriation bill, means that the emissions from 300–700 MW of thermal energy power in OPIC-financed projects will not be counted under the agency's GHG cap.

With respect to the overall size of OPIC's energy generation portfolio, however, we would note that OPIC is a small agency with a very limited number of deal teams. The absolute number of projects that can be financed and insured in any given year is constrained by this resource limitation. So while changes in OPIC's GHG emission reduction policy may shift the mix of power projects that are financed or insured, these changes are unlikely to expand the overall number of power projects that OPIC can support.

Question. You were asked about support for the off-grid light and power sector, but I do not think you answered the question. How has OPIC been able to use the ACEF program and other tools to serve this market? What are the prospects for further supporting off-grid businesses to dramatically increase power access?

Answer. Like other regions of the world, Africa needs of mix of power sources. On-grid, off-grid, urban and rural, renewable and base load power sources each make sense in specific environments and situations. But as a market-driven agency, OPIC is largely limited to the transactions that the private sector proposes.

Still, there are occasions when OPIC or partner agencies can strengthen the commercial viability of renewable energy proposals by providing a small increment of technical assistance—such as help in obtaining an engineering study, legal documentation, or an environmental impact statement—that would make the larger transaction more likely to achieve financial success. This need is particularly acute in smaller, off-grid, renewable energy projects.

This is a goal of the U.S.-Africa Clean Energy Finance Initiative (US–ACEF), which has been developed by OPIC, the State Department, and the U.S. Trade and Development Agency. Implementing ACEF is one of the key objectives of the Clean Energy Development & Finance Center in Johannesburg, South Africa, which is staffed by OPIC and USTDA representatives.

Here's what ACEF has provided so far:

ACEF Data (through 31 March 2014):
- Total Projects: 12
- Total Countries: 7
  - (Ethiopia, Kenya, Morocco, Namibia, Rwanda, Tanzania, Uganda)
- Power Africa Countries: 3
  - (Ethiopia, Kenya, Tanzania)
- Anticipated MW generated: 119
- Total Funds Approved: $6.23 M

While OPIC does not have a unique focus on off-grid solutions, it has supported a number of projects in this key market segment.

ACEF focuses specific attention on off-grid solutions. As of now, 6 of the 12 projects that ACEF has supported offer off-grid solutions. This will translate into an additional 23 MW of off-grid power generation in those countries (Ethiopia, Kenya, Morocco, Namibia, Rwanda, Tanzania, and Uganda). ACEF projects include both project financing and software approaches to promoting off-grid solutions.

And here's what ACEF's support looks like in the context of OPIC's overall Africa portfolio.

OPIC Exposure in Africa:

Total Exposure in Africa (as of 12/31/13): $3,977,195,067.12
Number of Finance Projects: 52
Number of Investment Funds Projects: 12
Number of Insurance Projects: 64
Total Number of OPIC Projects in Africa: 121
Renewable Energy commitments in Africa (FY12&13): $273 M
Renewable Energy commitments in Africa (FY08–13): $855 M

But ACEF cannot create projects out of whole cloth. To have the best chance of meeting the Power Africa and Electrify Africa goals, OPIC needs the authorities and flexibility to be responsive to commercially viable opportunities, such as a multiyear reauthorization and the increased staffing that would be enabled by the President's FY15 budget request.

Question. Congress gave OPIC statutory authority to make technical assistance grants to U.S. cooperatives and small businesses as part of its 1978 amendments to the Foreign Assistance Act. (Section 220 (a) and 2194 (e)). This authority gives OPIC broad discretion to use the agency's own income to make grants. How will OPIC use this authority to support the Power Africa initiative and deliver both increased access and sustainability?

Answer. While OPIC's authorization permits this activity, OPIC's appropriation does not fund its use. The modest technical assistance that OPIC is distributing through the ACEF program utilizes State Department funds. The use of these funds is stipulated in OPIC's agreement with the State Department. OPIC is therefore not using its own income for ACEF technical assistance.

RESPONSES OF HON. MIMI ALEMAYEHOU TO QUESTIONS SUBMITTED BY SENATOR BENJAMIN L. CARDIN

World Bank President Jim Yong Kim has said, "If we don't confront climate change, we won't end poverty." We understand that developing countries in Africa are relatively low—CO_2 emitting countries. We also understand that these countries need better access to electricity in order to become full partners in our global economy and to ensure effective delivery of social services, such as public health, education, and the like. This is going to require a delicate balance in our approach to PowerAfrica.

Question. How can we make sure that we reach the goal of providing electricity in underserved populations without compromising our climate change goals?

Answer. OPIC's renewable energy portfolio has been growing since 2007, and especially since 2009. In each of the last 3 years, OPIC has committed more than $1 billion to renewable energy projects. Partly because of OPIC's commitment to reduce greenhouse gas (GHG) emissions from its portfolio, but also because of rapidly growing market demand for renewable energy in emerging markets, OPIC's renewable energy commitments have dwarfed its thermal fuel commitments over the past 5 years.

OPIC's $1.5 billion commitment to Power Africa was premised in part on careful calculations of the GHG emissions that would be allowable under the reduction targets then in force. These GHG emissions should be sufficient to accommodate approximately 800 MW of thermal power production, in addition to the existing robust pipeline of renewable energy projects.

The Electrify Africa bill that has been approved by the House of Representatives contains more ambitious power generation and access goals than the Power Africa initiative. To achieve the Electrify Africa goals, OPIC would need the flexibility to finance a broader mix of energy. But it bears noting that OPIC, an inherently market-driven agency, has not financed a coal-fired power plant since 1996. This was more than a decade before the focus on renewable energy and the creation of the GHG emissions reduction plan.

OPIC anticipates that the suspension of its GHG emissions reduction goals in IDA-eligible countries for FY14, as mandated by the FY14 Omnibus Appropriation bill, means that the emissions from 300–700 MW of thermal energy power in OPIC-financed projects will not be counted under the agency's GHG cap.

With respect to the overall size of OPIC's energy generation portfolio, however, OPIC would note that it is a small agency with a very limited number of deal teams. The absolute number of projects that can be financed and insured in any given year is constrained by this resource limitation. So while changes in OPIC's GHG emission reduction policy may shift the mix of power projects that are financed or insured, these changes are unlikely to expand the overall number of power projects that OPIC can support.

Question. What has the administration done to limit the possible negative environmental impact of Power Africa?

Answer. For its part, OPIC maintains some of the most robust environmental standards among its development finance institution (DFI) peers. All projects that OPIC supports must meet rigorous environmental and social standards, over and above the GHG reduction targets. When OPIC's analysis suggests that a project may have significant negative environmental impacts, the project is opened to 30 days of public comment. In addition, OPIC proposes mitigation plans for all environmentally challenging projects. In many cases, adequate mitigation requires the installation of best available pollution controls. If these mitigants cannot be agreed upon with the project sponsors, OPIC will not go forward with the project. If the mitigants are agreed to and the project does go forward, it will be monitored on the ground by OPIC after the fact. OPIC conducts regular monitoring of all its projects, with particular attention to projects with higher environmental sensitivities. Environmental issues discovered during monitoring inspections must be rectified. Failure to do so can lead to a cessation of OPIC support, and/or the calling of the loan.

Question. The development of fossil fuels carries social and environmental costs over a range of areas: access to land, access to water, water pollution, air pollution and the resulting health impacts, and of course climate change. How have environmental and social assessments been incorporated into the choice of energy technology employed in the Power Africa Initiative's efforts?

Answer. Projects that OPIC supports must meet rigorous environmental and social standards. These include access to land and water and the protection of human health. OPIC helps investors identify opportunities to improve environmental performance and improve resilience in response to changing conditions. All projects are required to assess reasonable and feasible alternatives that would lower any environmental and social risks, including alternatives related to project location and selection of energy technology.

Question. How does it help Africa leap-frog forward toward a truly sustainable and efficient renewable energy based economy? Please describe any clean energy projects supported by the Initiative.

Answer. As noted above, OPIC has focused on renewable energy transactions in recent years. Thus, adapting this focus to Africa was a logical pivot. A summary of OPIC's African projects is below:

OPIC Exposure in Africa:
- Total Exposure in Africa (as of 12/31/13): $3,977,195,067.12
- Number of Finance Projects: 52
- Number of Investment Funds Projects: 12
- Number of Insurance Projects: 64
- Total Number of OPIC Projects in Africa: 121
- Renewable Energy commitments in Africa (FY12&13): $273 M
- Renewable Energy commitments in Africa (FY08–13): $855 M

In 2013, OPIC began its Africa Clean Energy Finance program in partnership with the State Department and USTDA. State provided OPIC with $15 million in funding (and USTDA with $5 million) in a 4-year program to target technical assistance financing to early state development of projects that might not otherwise occur without such backing. After establishing strong policies and procedures for the program, OPIC has committed financing to 12 projects for roughly $6 million in various renewable energy sectors. We expect to fully utilize the State Department transfer by the end of calendar year 2014. A summary of the ACEF program is below:

ACEF Data (to date):
- Total Projects: 12

Total Countries: 7
(Ethiopia, Kenya, Morocco, Namibia, Rwanda, Tanzania, Uganda)
Power Africa Countries: 3
(Ethiopia, Kenya, Tanzania)
Anticipated MW generated: 119
Total Funds Approved: $6.23 M

Examples of projects that are moving forward after just 1 year of ACEF technical assistance include: Gigawatt Global, an 8.5 MW solar project in Rwanda; Off-Grid Electric, which is distributing pay-as-you-go home solar systems in Tanzania; and Virunga Power, a 6 MW hydropower project in Kenya.

ACEF focuses specific attention on off-grid solutions. As of now, 6 of the 12 projects that ACEF has supported offer off-grid solutions. This will translate into 23 MW of off-grid power generation in those countries (Ethiopia, Kenya, Morocco, Namibia, Rwanda, Tanzania, and Uganda). ACEF projects include both project financing and software approaches to promoting off-grid solutions.

Overall, OPIC has a healthy pipeline of power projects that fall under Power Africa. The current pipeline of projects in development (not yet in implementation) includes roughly $1.7bn for over 2,000 MWs of power, two-thirds of which is thermal and one-third from renewable energy sources. This pipeline also includes a rich mix of on-grid and off-grid, renewable and thermal, urban and rural power.

Question. What benchmarks and metrics are set out to guide and evaluate Power Africa?

Answer. OPIC is working together with the interagency Monitoring and Evaluation Working Group for Power Africa to help establish benchmarks for the measuring the impacts of the Power Africa initiative. On its own, OPIC measures and monitors the impact on the ground of each of its private sector investments, including key impacts such as jobs created; additional local revenues generated; additional local purchasing, which can spur indirect job creation through supply chains; demonstration effects; and development reach, as products and services reach new, generally underserved populations.

Question. Is there a need to set some sort of cost-benefit ratio or criteria for authorizing Power Africa projects?

Answer. There are extensive metrics already being established for the program by the interagency Monitoring and Evaluation Working Group for Power Africa, an interagency group of experts on monitoring and evaluation.

But more broadly, every project that OPIC supports—in any sector and any country—undergoes rigorous scrutiny with regard to its costs and benefits.

This procedure, refined over decades of project finance experience, has enabled OPIC to select projects with the most development impact and the greatest likelihood of success.

The shorthand version of this analysis is called "the 4Rs," reflecting OPIC's emphases on risks, rewards, returns and resources.

Risks: The credit risks associated with the project are taken into careful account. These include not only transaction risk, but country risk, sector risk, counterparty risk, business plan risk, management risk, currency risk, credit history risk, and other financial risks of the project. Potential mitigants for each credit risk are also studied.

Development returns: OPIC analyzes (a) the developmental impact of the project, based on historically proven measures of local job creation, local procurement, worker training, demonstration effects of the project, positive environmental impact, broader economic impacts, etc., and (b) the U.S. impact of the project, based upon U.S. job creation, U.S. exports, balance of payment effects, capital mobilization, and market expansion for U.S. enterprises. In addition, the importance of the project to any relevant federal government initiatives (such as Power Africa) is taken into account.

Financial returns: OPIC also projects expected financial returns to the U.S. government and the taxpayers, weighing the financial risks associated with the project against the estimated interest spread, fees, and other financial returns.

Resources: The use of internal OPIC resources, given the complexity of the project and the dedicated OPIC personnel and funds needed to accomplish it, is likewise assessed. This includes OPIC staff resources that would be needed for such tasks as underwriting, legal analysis, document preparation, economic impact analysis, environmental assessments, portfolio tracking, and monitoring, in order to execute the project start to finish.

RESPONSES OF RICK ANGIUONI TO QUESTIONS SUBMITTED BY SENATOR CHRISTOPHER A. COONS

Question. What are Ex-Im's plans to meet its $5 billion commitment over the next 5 years to support Power Africa projects, do you see a commensurate increase in demand from the private sector, and what additional resources or authorities may be needed to ensure Ex-Im meets this commitment?

Answer. Ex-Im Bank is actively following more than a dozen projects in eight countries across sub-Saharan Africa. Most of these projects are in early-stage development. Ex-Im Bank continually engages the sponsors in the hope that sourcing comes from the United States and thus qualifies for our support. For example, Ex-Im Bank has entered into institutional arrangements with the Ministry of Power in Nigeria and Industrial Development Corp. of South Africa Ltd. (IDC). We plan to enter into additional strategic arrangements in the future to promote U.S. exports.

Given the above arrangements, coupled with various potential projects in the pipeline in countries such as Nigeria, Tanzania, Angola, Cote d'Ivoire, South Africa, Mozambique, Ghana, and Kenya, Ex-Im Bank sees strong growth in the power sector as well as other economic sectors such as aviation, transportation, oil and gas, mining, construction equipment, and health care.

Ex-Im Bank's Sub-Saharan Africa Advisory Committee (SAAC) is assisting Ex-Im in meeting its commitment to support Power Africa. Established by an Act of Congress, the Sub-Saharan Africa Advisory Committee (SAAC) provides guidance and advice regarding policies and programs designed to support the expansion of financial commitments by Ex-Im Bank in sub-Saharan Africa consistent with the Bank's mandates. This committee is comprised of members with extensive experience in Africa that can provide advice on strategy, financing, and marketing outreach.

Recognizing the massive investment needs of sub-Saharan Africa, U.S. companies are recognizing the potential for increased investments and exports to the region. Ex-Im Bank is aware of an increase in demand from the private sector and seeks to support those efforts. For example, some private sector companies that export to Africa are considering retooling their production facilities to source from the United States and create jobs in America. With respect to resources, Ex-Im appreciates the increase in appropriations for the Bank contained in the recent omnibus appropriations bill which will allow the Bank to invest in additional resources. Ex-Im Bank Senior Management is in the process of reviewing where to best place those resources.

Question. How does Ex-Im coordinate with the interagency to select and implement Power Africa projects, and do you coordinate with DOE to measure and evaluate the reliability of grid extension efforts?

Answer. The Bank actively participates with sister agencies in promoting power projects across the region. Working with the Department of Commerce, Ex-Im Bank works with the United States and Foreign Commercial Service, and actively supports the Doing Business in Africa campaign. The Bank participates in trade missions to identify opportunities and projects for financing. In countries where U.S. embassies do not have a U.S. and Foreign Commercial Service presence, Ex-Im works closely with the State Department's Econ/Commercial officers.

With the U.S. Trade and Development Agency (TDA) and Overseas Private Investment Corporation (OPIC), Ex-Im Bank is engaged in the U.S.-Africa Clean Energy Development and Finance Center (Center). The Center is an initiative by USTDA, OPIC, and Ex-Im Bank to provide a coordinated approach to clean energy project development in sub-Saharan Africa. Specifically with TDA, Ex-Im participates in Reverse Trade Missions where we highlight the Bank's financing in support of U.S. exports for prospective African purchasers of American-made equipment.

Ex-Im Bank actively participates in the weekly Power Africa Working Group meetings which have representation across agencies including OPIC, USTDA, USAID, State, Department of Energy (DOE), Army Corps of Engineers, National Security Council (NSC), Commerce, African Development Foundation (ADF), Millennium Challenge Corporation (MCC), and Treasury.

Ex-Im Bank does not coordinate with DOE to evaluate and measure grid extension efforts. This is because the scope of the work is more developmental and of a technical assistance nature. As a financing institution with a mandate to finance U.S. exports, technical assistance is not part of Ex-Im's mandate.

RESPONSES OF RICK ANGIUONI TO QUESTIONS
SUBMITTED BY SENATOR BENJAMIN L. CARDIN

Question. What benchmarks and metrics are set out to guide and evaluate Power Africa?

Answer. Ex-Im Bank pledged support of up to $5 billion over the next 5 years in support of the President's Power Africa Initiative. The Bank's $5 billion pledge is a signal to African countries and investors in the African power sector that they should source equipment and services from the United States.

Ex-Im Bank is actively following more than a dozen possible power projects across sub-Saharan Africa. Most of these projects are in early-stage development. Ex-Im Bank continually engages the sponsors in the hopes that sourcing comes from the United States and thus qualifies for Ex-Im support.

Ex-Im Bank is demand-driven and reviews projects and applications as they come into the Bank. Ex-Im Bank's mission is to support U.S. jobs through exports by supporting the U.S. content of exports. The Bank works with project sponsors, developers, engineering, procurement and contracting (EPC) firms, and with original equipment manufacturers (OEMs) in financing U.S. exports for power projects.

In terms of tracking progress toward Power Africa's goals, Ex-Im works closely with USAID which, as the Secretariat for Power Africa, is responsible for coordinating and tracking of progress toward the two overarching goals of Power Africa: an additional 10,000 MWs of additional generation capacity added to the power grid and an additional 20 million households and businesses connected to the power grid.

Question. Is there a need to set some sort of cost-benefit ratio or criteria for authorizing Power Africa projects?

Answer. Ex-Im Bank's mission is to support U.S. jobs through exports. The Bank's financing is done at no net cost to the U.S. taxpayer (we actually generated more than $1 billion in deficit reducing receipts in FY 2013), and we maintain an overall default rate of approximately one-quarter of a percent. (This default rate is different than the default rates published in the annual Budget Appendix due to differing definitions. The reported rate in the Budget Appendix reflects projected defaults over the life of the loan while the default rate in this report reflects actual defaults at a particular point in time.)

Ex-Im Bank financing supports exports of U.S. goods and services. There are varying levels of job intensity in the exports that Ex-Im finances ranging from manufactured to technical engineering services for a power projects. If a buyer in a foreign country receives a loan to purchase U.S. goods, we meet our mission of supporting U.S. jobs. Ex-Im Bank's financing supported an estimated 1.2 million jobs over the past 5 years, including 205,000 jobs in FY 2013 alone.

Ex-Im Bank's congressional mandate to support exports to sub-Saharan Africa must be undertaken consistent with the Bank's reasonable assurance of repayment mandate, our environmental guidelines, and with Ex-Im Bank's mission to create and sustain U.S. jobs.

Ex-Im Bank is transactional/project driven. All projects, including those in the power sector, need to be bankable; they are thus, subject to our normal due diligence process (financial/technical/environmental) to ensure each meets Ex-Im Bank's mandated criteria of reasonable assurance of repayment.

RESPONSES OF RICK ANGIUONI TO QUESTIONS
SUBMITTED BY SENATOR BOB CORKER

Question. I have heard reports from constituents concerned that, because of perceived commercial risks, limits have been placed on Ex-Im's Working Capital Guarantee Program (WCGP) for the following countries: Argentina, Ghana, Indonesia, Mauritania, Tanzania, and Zambia. As you know, Ghana and Tanzania are Power Africa countries.

- Could you describe any limits placed on lending to businesses exporting to these countries and, if so, please provide the reasons why?

Answer. Ex-Im Bank's cover policy (terms and conditions of doing business in a particular market) is contained in a document known as the Country Limitation Schedule (CLS), and is available to all exporters by visiting our Web site. Ex-Im Bank determines its cover policy for each market based on the country risk ratings approved through the Interagency Country Risk Assessment System (''ICRAS'') chaired by the Office of Management and Budget (OMB).

Based on the level of risk reflected by such ratings and in consideration of the mandate to have a reasonable assurance of repayment in the commitments that it incurs, Ex-Im Bank may decide to open or close in a particular market. Where open, Ex-Im Bank may decide to have certain restrictions, such as typically requiring a bank guarantee or a sovereign guarantee, that are reflected in notes 1 through 14 in the Country Limitation Schedule. The underwriting of transactions must be in accord with the Bank's cover policy as per the CLS. For example, in Mauritania, Ex-Im Bank is open only for short-term public and private sector business (up to 180 day terms; exceptionally 360 days) pursuant to its Africa initiative; closed under its normal programs for longer terms for all public and private sector business and notes 1, 11a, 11b, and 13 apply. Any additional limits and/or conditions are based on an assessment of the risk related to a specific transaction.

Ex-Im Bank does provide some additional flexibility for private sector working capital transactions in Ghana, Tanzania, Zambia, and Indonesia that are subject to a requirement of a bank guarantee or high quality financial information. The standard policy for working capital transactions allows for the substitution of an irrevocable letter of credit in place of a bank guarantee. In addition, Ex-Im Bank will consider on a case-by-case basis other nonbank guaranteed transactions. The standard policy for working capital transactions subject to high quality financial information, also allows for the substitution of an irrevocable letter of credit. In addition, exceptions may also be made for transactions that are insured for comprehensive political and commercial risk.

Question. I have heard from small business exporters concerns about Ex-Im's ''reduction clause.'' I understand the importance of securing deals with collateral requirements. I also understand that Ex-Im Bank's working capital guarantees depend on having adequate collateral in the form of raw materials, finished goods, accounts receivables, and other specified assets and that there might be a need to condition loan disbursements, supported by inventory, by capping at a certain amount. However, I am hearing concerns that the Working Capital Guarantee Program's reduction clause is unreasonably limiting the ability of small exporters, who are dependent on securing loans with inventory and that this clause, as currently interpreted by Ex-Im, may be undermining Ex-Im's goal of assisting small business exporters and instead creating an unfair disadvantage to small businesses.

- Can you provide me with further detail on the workings of the reduction clause? Is it an accurate interpretation to say that no more than 60 percent of actual disbursements can be supported by inventory? Please explain, in detail, why this is or is not the case.

Answer. The reduction clause referred to above is Ex-Im Bank's general policy with respect to Working Capital Revolving Loan Facilities (other than Transaction Specific Revolving Loan Facilities), is that at no time shall the portion of the principal balance of the credit accommodations that is supported by export-related inventory exceed 60 percent of the sum of the outstanding disbursements plus the aggregate undrawn face value of all outstanding Commercial Letters of Credit. At least 40 percent of the total principal balance must consist of export-related accounts receivable.

Ex-Im Bank recognizes that from time to time it may be necessary for a small business exporter to carry inventory balances that exceed 60 percent. This often happens when export sales are growing, and more inventory is needed to fill orders. To accommodate this need and facilitate the export, Ex-Im Bank on a case-by-case basis, will allow the percentage of export-related inventory to exceed 60 percent of the outstanding principal balance. Our approval to allow the percentage of export-related inventory to exceed 60 percent is based on an assessment of risk related to each specific transaction.

RESPONSES OF HON. EARL GAST TO QUESTIONS
SUBMITTED BY SENATOR CHRISTOPHER A. COONS

Question. How can the administration more effectively coordinate with Congress to ensure the Power Africa initiative is funded, authorized, and sustained in the future?

Answer. The administration appreciates the committee's engagement and support of Power Africa. We believe that your continued focus and support on the important issue of increasing access to energy in Africa through briefings and hearings will help ensure the Initiative's long-term sustainability. Congressional support for the President's FY 2015 request for the Development Assistance account where funding for Power Africa is allocated will be essential. Additionally, we hope that Congress will continue to identify and create opportunities to mobilize support for Power Africa by hosting events in the U.S.—similar to the very successful ''Opportunity Africa

Conference'' recently held in Delaware. These events provide a forum for us to speak to businesses, constituents, the diaspora, and technical experts about the goals, progress, and implementation of Power Africa. We also welcome opportunities for congressional and staff delegations to visit Power Africa sites in Africa where they can meet with our transaction advisors and our teams and partners in the field. Additionally, bicameral and bipartisan legislation which support the goals of Power Africa will signal congressional interest in the sustainability and future of the Initiative.

Question. Latin America and Asia have substantially accelerated their energy production, resulting in electrification rates upward of 70 percent in most areas. What are the lessons learned from these other low- and middle-income countries with regards to tackling electrification challenges in sub-Saharan Africa and ensuring sustainability of the Power Africa Initiative in the long term?

Answer. A fundamental lesson from Latin America and Asia is that if the legal and regulatory structure is in place for electrification projects to recoup their investments that the incentives for a wide variety of approaches play a huge role in improving overall access. We have also seen a number of small-scale renewable models that demonstrate that these power projects can be bankable and sustainable. It is critical that the tariff structures are in place so that costs of producing the power are fully reflected. In addition, the legal and regulatory structure needs to be transparent and predictable over time so that investors have a high level of confidence that they can recoup their investment over time. There must be clarity as to whom the power can be sold, how that power is sold and at what price. For power projects, this needs to be clear not only for the immediate term, but extending forward for 25 years given the size of investments needed for power generation projects. Additionally, we have seen important progress in developing sustainable business models for small scale and distributed energy solutions deployed in underserved areas due to improvements in low cost technology. These solutions are particularly important in providing access to power in areas that are not expected to be connected to the power grid in the near to medium term. For example, we have seen impressive advancements in Bangladesh deploying lower cost, technology appropriate solar power solutions such as those through Grameen Shakti. Households take out micro-credit loans for small solar systems and are able to repay the loan resulting from cost savings realized by replacing higher cost energy sources such as kerosene.

Question. We understand that additional funding would be required to add countries beyond the initial six focus countries. What plans exist to consider the future expansion of Power Africa beyond the six focus countries, and how much additional cost would that require?

Answer. The initial set of six countries was chosen after extensive analysis conducted by the U.S. Government. Around 40 percent of the population without access to electricity in sub-Saharan Africa live in these six countries according to a 2013 OECD/IEA report. Given the needs across the continent, USAID and other USG agencies are also working in other countries like South Africa, Mozambique, and Malawi; and other donors are playing a significant role too. With the great deal of interest in Power Africa and as this model is tested and proven, we may look to expand our efforts.

The administration has sufficiently funded Power Africa to meet its current goals with those six countries. To meet the President's commitment, USAID has identified $285 million of funding for Power Africa to coordinate and provide technical assistance. Technical assistance supports power generation, distribution, and transmission projects, including clean energy projects and off-grid and mini-grid solutions. Assistance is also being provided to strengthen the enabling environment for private investment, including legal and regulatory frameworks and host country institutional capacity.

Currently, the President's Power Africa goal is 10,000 MW in six focus countries, however, in order to meet goals identified in the House Electrify Africa bill of 20,000 MW, new countries would need to be added as Power Africa would need to expand the universe of potential new energy transactions, and each country has limited absorption capacity for new power. The Power Africa model will be severely constrained to expand to new focus countries without additional resources.

We estimate a properly resourced focus country costs approximately $20 million/year for USAID, a cost that includes delivery units, off-shore transaction advisors, technical support, legal support, in-country embassy staff, senior advisors group, off-grid solutions, and monitoring and evaluation. Additional resources for regional activities such as support for geothermal energy, the U.S. Africa Clean Energy Fund and small scale and distributed energy efforts are needed to help advance our overall objectives.

Question. What are some of the challenges for U.S. energy companies doing business in Tanzania, where the government-owned utility is insolvent? What measures is the Power Africa team considering to help Tanzania address this issue and ensure U.S. companies do not suffer as a result of TANESCO's arrears?

Answer. TANESCO has grappled with payment arrears and liquidity issues, created by operational inefficiencies and tariffs that did not fully capture the cost of providing power to its customers. As these arrears built up over time, TANESCO has not had the liquidity to make payments to power generation companies, including American-owned companies. However, there has been significant engagement by donors to help TANESCO and the Government of Tanzania address these issues impacting its liquidity and arrears. We have started to see TANESCO take concrete steps to address these liquidity and arrears issues. TANESCO recently announced a plan to make payments and reduce the outstanding arrears by the end of 2015 by increasing operational efficiencies, directing increased revenues from the increased tariff increase to cost reflective levels and reduce the cost of generation by bringing cheaper power sources online. Under Power Africa, USAID and MCC are working closely with the GOT and other donors such as the World Bank and DFID to strengthen power sector institutions and the legal and regulatory environment. TANESCO is starting to show some progress in increasing its collections and liquidity. However, TANESCO will need to continue progress in improving its operational efficiencies and implement a phased restructuring to unbundle generation, transmission and distribution lines of its business.

Question. Are we fully leveraging the strengths of the other partner agencies, such as the Department of Energy, which is among the best equipped with expertise relevant to the energy sector? Are there ways to better utilize the expertise and draw in other federal and nongovernmental assets such as the DOE's national labs, U.S. universities, and faith based groups to support the greater Power Africa mission?

Answer. We are working to fully leverage the strengths of other partner agencies. The Power Africa Working Group or PAWG is fairly simple in its organization and implementation, but has been effective in its implementation due to the commitment of all 12 Power Africa agencies including the Department of Energy. USAID serves as the Secretariat for Power Africa—supporting the leadership of the White House for the Initiative as a catalyst and facilitator. Agency roles and responsibilities are defined by the tools and comparative strengths of each agency. For example, OPIC, Ex-IM and USAID through the Development Credit Authority provide financing tools; the State Department provides leadership and support through its principal officers at Post and in Washington in the diplomatic space and through initiatives such as Sustainable Energy 4 All (SE4All); State, MCC, and USAID provide support for policy and institutional reforms in the power sector; the Department of Energy, U.S. African Development Foundation and USAID provide critical support for renewable technologies as well as off grid and minigrid solutions and approaches. We continue to explore opportunities to engage US. Universities and faith based groups, national labs to support and accomplish the goals of Power Africa. In addition, Power Africa serves as a one-stop shop for the private sector through which they can access multiple points of contacts at the 12 U.S. agencies through the Power Africa Secretariat. Additionally, Power Africa is in the process of embedding liaisons from OPIC, the Export-Import Bank, the Department of Energy, the Department of Commerce and USTDA in the Coordinators office in order to strengthen the reach back to the tools and resources in these agencies.

There is no "one size fits all" solution to Africa's energy challenges, so Power Africa is serving as a conduit for pooling the expertise of the U.S. Government and other donors such as the World Bank and African Development Bank to tailor solutions to address each country's and each project's unique challenges. Power Africa is using a transaction-centered approach that concentrates on closing those deals that will have the greatest impact on improving sustainable energy access. The approach provides host governments, the private sector, and donors with incentives to encourage collaboration, provide quick results, and drive systemic reforms that will facilitate future investment.

One example of this is a recent meeting in Washington where top U.S. and African energy lawyers who have negotiated power purchasing agreements in many of the Power Africa countries gathered at the U.S. Department of Commerce alongside experts from international financial institutions and lawyers from Power Africa governments for a workshop hosted by the Commercial Law Development Program. Their goal was to emerge with annotated, standard power purchasing agreement clauses that will significantly reduce the amount of time spent on negotiating the terms of power deals. In short, this will help electricity come online more quickly.

Question. Within the Power Africa Initiative, USAID is charged with increasing private and other investment for small-scale, clean energy projects, including distributed generation, off-grid or minigrid development projects, and provide support to rural electrification initiatives. Please provide more information about the specific strategies USAID plans to employ to accomplish this mission, as well as progress toward achieving these goals?

Answer. As a whole, the region has tremendous untapped potential for sustainable energy generation. For example, East Africa's Rift Valley alone has the potential to produce up to 15,000 MW of geothermal energy, which could provide future generations with a sustainable, dependable supply of electricity. Power Africa is providing a significant amount of support to develop Africa's geothermal resources and large-scale wind generation. For example, two of the largest transactions in Kenya will use wind turbines to generate power.

In addition, minigrid and off-grid solutions, ranging from small and independent solar powered networks serving 200 homes to stand alone hydroelectric power systems to biodigesters which produce electricity, could effectively and affordably provide energy access to communities—often allowing them to ''leap frog'' traditional grid extension and level the playing field between rural and urban communities.

Although Africa only produces 6 percent of global greenhouse gas emissions, no country has developed its energy supply without using a mix of renewable and fossil fuel energy sources. Expanding energy access generally requires deploying a mix of the best available generation resources and fuels. A large number of African countries have large reserves of natural gas, a fuel that results in 47 percent less greenhouse gas emissions compared to coal-fired power plants. This is underscored by the fact that more than two-thirds of the population of sub-Saharan Africa is without electricity, and more than 85 percent of those living in rural areas lack access.

Without access to reliable energy sources, most African businesses now rely on costly and high-emission kerosene or diesel generators to power their businesses. As they grow, so does pollution. Annually, Nigeria loses $2 billion of potential revenue through natural gas flaring—a process that not only negatively impacts Nigeria's economy, but also creates significant greenhouse gas emissions.

Power Africa is pursuing activities that encourage clean energy projects, energy efficiency, low-carbon energy development, and energy sector reforms.

The Off-Grid Challenge, for instance, is a partnership between the U.S. African Development Foundation and General Electric that asked for ideas—from companies or from individuals—to develop or scale up off-grid activities that would reach communities not served by existing power grids. Six first-round winners were selected based on the sustainability, efficiency, and impact of their projects. One Off-Grid Challenge winner, Mibawa Suppliers, will expand delivery of pay-as-you-go lighting to households in rural Kenya. Another, GVE Projects Ltd., will electrify off-grid communities using metered solar and rechargeable battery systems. However, Power Africa's off-grid solutions are not about identifying one-off projects that may not be scalable due to the lack of interest on the part of large investors. For this reason, Power Africa continues to explore opportunities to bundle together off-grid projects so that institutional investors can deploy capital into these projects at scale.

RESPONSES OF HON. EARL GAST TO QUESTIONS
SUBMITTED BY SENATOR ROBERT MENENDEZ

Question #1. In your testimony, you stated that you are hoping to help the off-grid lighting and power market achieve greater scale. The International Finance Corporation (IFC) is looking to create a fund to supply low-cost, patient capital to firms scaling up production and distribution of off-grid renewable energy products.

- Is that effort something Power Africa plans on assisting with? To date, has there been any communication between Power Africa and the IFC concerning this effort?

Answer. Power Africa has been heavily engaged with the IFC regarding the development of the Lighting Africa Trade Finance Facility. We are also collaborating with IFC on a number of other activities. Power Africa and IFC's Lighting Africa overlap in four countries: Ethiopia, Kenya, Nigeria, and Tanzania therefore there is great potential for collaboration.

Moreover, Power Africa has been heavily engaged with the World Bank on a broader effort to align activities, including those of the IFC. Since last summer, we have been working closely with the World Bank and the IFC at their headquarters and on the country level to identify areas of collaboration and identify key activities on which Power Africa and the World Bank will partner. We are in the process of finalizing a Memorandum of Understanding to formalize these areas of collaboration. We anticipate a formal announcement of this partnership in the near future.

Question #2. You cite the Off-Grid Challenge in your testimony. This innovative program will help achieve the laudable goal of developing new businesses and new business models. Similarly USAID has used the Development Credit Authority (DCA) to help emerging off-grid companies get off the ground. But what about businesses which already have proven business models and are ready to grow rapidly? What can USAID do to help existing successful off-grid companies scale up?

Answer. Power Africa is developing an initiative-wide strategy for mini-grid and off-grid power focused on fostering and scaling up clean and hybrid energy solutions in partnership with impact investors, existing successful off-grid companies, and other organizations active in this space. Through financial and technical support, the strategy will seek to test and invest in different business and project models, identifying technically and financially sustainable solutions for small scale energy. The strategy is twofold: (1) mobilizing finance and (2) strengthening institutions, policy frameworks, and quality assurance. Illustrative activities include:

1. Partnerships with impact investors and practitioners to mobilize financing, mitigate risk, and provide targeted technical assistance through USAID Global Development Alliances, DCA facilities, Development Innovation Ventures, and other funds.
2. Financial and technical assistance for small and medium enterprises to innovate and scale through the Africa Clean Energy Fund implemented by OPIC and USTDA, and USADF/GE's Off-Grid Energy Challenge with USAID support.
3. Development and implementation of a quality assurance framework for mini-grids through the Department of Energy and National Renewable Energy Laboratory (NREL) partnership.
4. Capacity building and transaction advisory services for rural and renewable energy agencies.

Question #3. USAID's DCA has been successful in helping new off-grid companies such as M–KOPA establish themselves, but DCA provides loan guarantees for less than 30 projects a year, worldwide, across all sectors.

- What can be done to increase the number of DCA loan guarantees in total, and to off-grid entrepreneurs in particular?
- In the hearing, you cited your proposal to increase the cap, but, at best, won't that result in just a few more loan guarantees?
- How do we double or triple the number of loan guarantees for the promising off-grid lighting and power sector?

Answer. While DCA provides loan guarantee for about 30 projects per year, the size and scale of those projects have significantly increased over the past 2 years. The office expanded from $200 million in mobilized capital (through 31 transactions) in FY 2011 to $500 million in mobilized capital (through 26 transactions) in FY 2013. To significantly increase the size and number of transactions in future years and, to be consistent with the goals outlined in the Electrify Africa Act of 2014 (H.R. 2548), DCA would need an increase of its loan guarantee cap from the current $1.5 billion per year to $2 billion per year. This increase will accommodate much larger and more catalytic deals, particularly with respect to Power Africa transactions. With current resources in FY 2014, DCA anticipates the closing of 20 transactions in Africa, of which 5 will be in power. With the increased cap, both the number of guarantees and the amount financed could increase significantly.

It should be noted that financing is not the sole means to increase these loan guarantees; improvements to the business climate are essential as well. Power Africa includes assistance to a range of local partners to strengthen institutions and build capacity of public and private sector stakeholders, including local financial institutions, to absorb available financing and to make these projects successful.

Questions #4 & #5. So far, the Power Africa Initiative seems intensely focused on attracting private capital to centralized power plants. That is obviously an essential part of the equation in expanding economic opportunity and electricity access throughout sub-Saharan Africa, but the plan for actually expanding access to electricity seems more vague.

- Will a clearer plan emerge?

In the past, we have seen international support for centralized power plants built to serve particular extractive industries that do little or nothing to provide increased access to electricity for people.

◆ Given the emphasis on centralized generation in the Power Africa Initiative, how can we be sure we are paying enough attention to electricity access?

Answer. In addition to Power Africa's generation goal, Power Africa aims to increase connections for 20 million households or commercial entities. Large generation projects are not a comprehensive solution on a continent that remains largely rural, where national grids neither extend to rural areas nor have sufficient generation capacity. Therefore, increasing access to reliable and affordable electricity through both grid-based and off-grid solutions is essential for poverty eradication and economic growth. In order to accomplish our access goals, we are focused on expanding the distribution of power, enhancing the affordability of power by reducing technical and financial losses, and increasing access through mini-grid and off-grid projects as part of, and in addition to, the mini- and off-grid strategy described above (Question 2), illustrative activities include:

- Technical assistance to Ghana and Tanzania's utilities to reduce losses and improve efficiency, thereby improving access and affordability.
- Policy and political engagement on their national electricity legislation, policies, and sector planning to align resources and projects with access goals.
- Funding for Liberia's utility to extend the grid in Monrovia to increase connections.

To ensure we are paying enough attention to electricity access, Power Africa also considers a set of factors related to access when selecting its priority generation transactions to support with USG resources, including:

- Primary Impact: The project increases availability, access, or efficiency/reliability of electric power in the country;
- Catalytic Impact: Project has potential for scalability, replicability, or demonstration impact;
- Clean Energy Resources: Project prioritizes emission reduction, renewable energy and/or energy efficiency technologies to improve quality and mix of electric power in the country;
- Private Sector Role: Project catalyzes private sector participation or investment;
- Project Viability: Project is viable in terms of bankability, affordability, technical merit, environmental/social impact, and timeline.

Question #6. I would like to better understand Power Africa's plan to double access to electricity in sub-Saharan Africa. Power Africa is described as a private sector, transaction-based program, but, at least at this point, most businesses are not interested in investing in power lines or distribution lines in Power Africa countries.

◆ How does USAID plan to address areas where access to electric service remains extremely low?

◆ How will it address the fact that connecting new customers can actually lose utilities money because new customers often use little energy at first?

◆ What role does USAID see for rural communities with respect to ownership, governance and management of rural electric systems?

◆ What specific objectives does USAID believe must be accomplished in order to link increased access to commercial electric service with job creation, income generation, and support for small business and food security?

Answer. To improve access to electricity in sub-Saharan Africa, Power Africa is taking a country-specific approach to address challenges associated with electric service distribution; leveraging individual transactions to advance economic growth; and launching the aforementioned mini- and off-grid strategy to improve access. This strategy explores opportunities and methods to scale up various kinds of models (such as anchor clients, prepaid electricity models, and smart metering) within rural and remote contexts. Moreover, the off-grid and mini-grid strategy will also support other development objectives for which energy access is critical. This includes electricity for health clinics, street-light safety, and home and small enterprise uses.

Objectives and accompanying activities include:

- Helping state-owned distribution companies improve their performance and viability. For example, in Ghana we launched a change management program to improve the Electricity Company of Ghana's functions.
- Improving private sector investment and participation in distribution. For example, in Nigeria, USAID is supporting Nigeria's privatization process of 10 distribution companies through technical assistance and financing. The improved management of the distribution sector will improve the quality of service and lead to more connected customers as privatized companies expand their oper-

ations. USAID is also working in Ghana, in concert with MCC, to share positive privatization experiences and lessons learned in electricity distribution.

- Aligning and leveraging energy transactions with local economic growth and development opportunities.
  - In Kenya, Power Africa recently helped launch a 10 MW biomass project with Cummins that will use mesquite wood, a highly invasive species, as feedstock for its generator. This plant is a source of both energy and income for local residents who now will sell the wood for fuel at four times the price they currently sell for charcoal. Power Africa helped facilitate the power purchasing agreement negotiations between Cummins—a U.S. company—and the Government of Kenya. Cummins is looking to expand to add up to 18 new biomass projects in Kenya and exploring opportunities in other Power Africa partner countries.
  - In Tanzania, Power Africa Transaction Advisors are supporting several renewable energy generation projects linked to addressing the vital constraints of adequate and reliable power for agricultural production and processing in the Southern Agriculture Corridor, a key geographic focus for Feed the Future. Projects including a Husk Power model for small-scale, distributed generation based on processing waste products such as rice husks or other biomass feed-stocks from FTF value chains, and small hydro projects to increase generation potential in the corridor.

Regarding the role of communities in rural electrification, USAID supports community consultation on projects as well as models for communities owning, operating, and maintaining power systems. At the project level, USAID, and all USG agencies, are guided by environmental regulations and best practices which explicitly include community consultation during the project development process. USAID implementing partners are required under their agreements with USAID to specifically assess and incorporate the impact of youth and gender in their technical assistance approach, emphasizing the importance of underrepresented elements of communities in the design, implementation, and outcomes of these efforts.

Much of our assistance requires community engagement far beyond consultation, especially when local partners and stakeholders play a direct role in project implementation. For example, in Liberia, Power Africa is supporting the establishment of local community cooperatives to own and operate renewable energy microgrids. Through the U.S. African Development Fund and GE's Off Grid Challenge, Power Africa awarded six $100,000 grants to support sustainable renewable power generation initiatives at the community level. For example, one awardee, Kenyan suppliers will expand delivery of pay-as-you-go lighting options to households in rural areas, while another awardee, TransAfrica Gas and Electric, will power cold storage facilities with solar systems for farmers and fishermen. Awardee Afrisol Energy's biodigester will produce electricity for small businesses in Nairobi's urban settlements. The Off Grid Challenge has enabled a high level of innovation and community participation, and will be expanded to all six Power Africa countries later this year with USAID support.

RESPONSE OF HON. EARL GAST TO QUESTION
SUBMITTED BY SENATOR BOB CORKER

Question. As we know, a significant number of Africans live in rural areas and lack access to electricity. Power Africa could be an important solution to address Africa's energy poverty and could deliver immediate progress.

- How does USAID plan to address rural areas where access to electric service remains extremely low? And, what role does USAID see for rural communities with respect to ownership, governance, and management of rural electric systems?

Answer. USAID plans to increase access in rural areas where access to electric service remains extremely low in large part through Power Africa Initiative. USAID recognizes the important role that rural communities play with respect to the ownership, governance and management of rural electric systems. Reaching the most inaccessible corners of Africa's rural communities and other underserved populations is a critical component of Power Africa. Decentralized off-grid and mini-grid solutions often offer the swiftest, cleanest, and most innovative solutions to energy poverty by sidestepping the need to connect to the national electricity network. To accomplish our goals for increased access, we are focused on expanding the distribution of power, enhancing the affordability of power and increasing access through mini-grid and off-grid projects. Given the constraints to expanding access through grid extension alone, the Power Africa Initiative is aligning new and existing small scale activities under a more targeted framework: an initiative-wide strategy for mini-grid and off-grid power that will bring together the tools, expertise and resources available from the 12 partner U.S. Government Agencies. This strategy builds on existing efforts by multilateral agencies, U.S. Government initiatives, the private sector, NGOs, and other practitioners to address issues around energy access and will foster clean and renewable energy solutions.

Additionally, through financial and technical support, the Power Africa strategy will test and invest in different business and project models, identifying technically and financially sustainable solutions for small scale energy. The strategy will focus on two main components: Policy and Quality Assurance Framework and Finance. Activities under the strategy are expected to include:

1. Institutional, policy and regulatory planning, development and reform focused on off-grid and mini-grid development. Building public sector capacity that enables or promotes private sector small-scale project development and investment will improve the public sector's capacity to act as an effective counterpart. This can be done through the development of the capacity of rural energy agencies and associations and technical/transaction advice to the private sector. For example, a Power Africa transaction advisor is embedded in Tanzania's Rural and Renewable Energy Agency to identify and advance policy reform issues and generation transactions;
2. Provision of market information and activities that support the private sector's understanding of business opportunities and regulatory processes;
3. Developing and implementing quality assurance frameworks for mini-grids through the Department of Energy and National Renewable Energy Laboratory (NREL) partnership;
4. Providing financial and technical assistance for Small and Medium Enterprises innovation and scaling (Africa Clean Energy Fund implemented by OPIC and USTDA, Off-Grid Energy Challenge);
5. Catalyzing increased private sector investment for small-scale projects with credible developers and sustainable business models through risk mitigation, technical assistance, and finance (via USAID Global Development Alliances and Development Credit Authority facilities, OPIC investment in funds or directly into companies);
6. Partnering with impact investors and practitioners in the mini-grid and off-grid space to mobilize financial resources combined with targeted technical expertise (USAID Global Development Alliances).

Additionally, USAID supports community consultation on projects as well as models for communities owning, operating, and maintaining power systems. Power Africa also encourages host country partners to develop protocols at the regulatory and utility levels to protect consumer rights, facilitate public/community participation in regulatory processes, and conduct outreach on issues such as tariff changes.

At the project level, USAID, and all USG agencies, are guided by environmental regulations and best practices which explicitly include community consultation during the project development process. USAID implementing partners are required under their agreements with USAID to specifically assess and incorporate the impact of youth and gender in their technical assistance approach, emphasizing the importance of underrepresented elements of communities in the design, implementation, and outcomes of these efforts.

Much of our assistance requires community engagement far beyond consultation, especially when local partners and stakeholders play a direct role in project implementation. For example, in Liberia, Power Africa is supporting the establishment of local community cooperatives to own and operate renewable energy microgrids.

The Off-Grid Challenge is a partnership between the U.S. African Development Foundation and General Electric that asked for ideas—from companies or from individuals—to develop or scale up off-grid activities that would reach communities not served by existing power grids, including rural communities. Six first-round winners were selected based on the sustainability, efficiency, and impact of their projects and awarded $100,000 grants in Nigeria and Kenya.

- Solar World (E.A.) Ltd. will construct 5 solar water points to provide water and electricity in semiarid areas;
- Afrisol Energy's biodigester will produce electricity for small businesses in Nairobi's urban settlements;
- Mibawa Suppliers will expand delivery of pay-as-you-go lighting to households in rural Kenya;
- TransAfrica Gas and Electric will power cold storage facilities with solar systems for farmers and fisherman;

- GVE Projects Ltd. will electrify off-grid communities using metered solar and rechargeable battery systems;
- Afe Babalola University will investigate a hydroelectric and solar system to serve students and faculty. One Off-Grid Challenge winner, Mibawa Suppliers, will expand delivery of pay-as-you-go lighting to households in rural Kenya. Another, GVE Projects Ltd., will electrify off-grid communities using metered solar and rechargeable battery systems.

However, Power Africa's off-grid solutions are not about identifying one-off projects that may not be scalable due to the lack of interest on the part of large investors. For this reason, Power Africa continues to explore opportunities to bundle off-grid projects so that institutional investors can deploy capital into these projects at scale.

In Kenya, Power Africa recently helped launch a 10 megawatt biomass project with Cummins that will use mesquite wood, a highly invasive species, as feedstock for its generator. This plant is a source of both energy and income for local community residents who now will sell the wood for fuel at four times the price they currently sell for charcoal. Power Africa helped facilitate the power purchasing agreement negotiations between Cummins—a U.S. company—and the Government of Kenya. Cummins is looking to expand to add up to 18 new biomass projects in Kenya and exploring opportunities in other Power Africa partner countries. Through the U.S.-Africa Clean Energy Financing Facility, Power Africa also provided grants to support a 5.6 megawatt mini-grid biomass project in Tanzania and a grant used for software design and supply chain management for pay-as-you-go solar home systems in rural Tanzania.

USAID vis-a-vis Power Africa is committed to increasing access to electric service in rural areas and acknowledges the important role that rural communities play in reaching the Initiative's goal of increasing electricity access by adding more than 60 million new household and business connections.

Responses of Hon. Earl Gast to Questions Submitted by Senator Benjamin L. Cardin

Question. There has been an increasing recognition in the public and private sectors of the critical need for involvement of local impacted communities. In addition to basic consultation, projects are more sustainable when they go beyond consultation to create an environment where local communities are active participants in all stages of planning and implementation.

- How will Power Africa ensure that the impact on local communities—particularly land and livelihoods—are evaluated and shared prior to project implementation?
- What structures exist to guarantee community participation throughout the process and how can they be strengthened?

Answer. Power Africa uses an innovative private-sector-based approach to accelerate the planning and completion of both large and small power projects in sub-Saharan Africa. These projects have a broad range of stakeholders, including local communities, businesses, financial institutions, government institutions, and others. Power Africa's central premise is that public/private partnerships, based on shared goals and objectives, will also drive the six focus countries to develop the necessary infrastructure as well as the institutional, regulatory and human resources needed to increase the availability of power and attract the investment resources needed to grow each country's power sector.

USAID, the State Department, the Millennium Challenge Corporation (MCC) and other U.S. Government agencies support community consultation. MCC has specific requirements for community and nongovernmental organization consultation in their country compact development process. Power Africa also supports host country partners to develop protocols at the regulatory and utility levels to protect consumer rights, facilitate public participation in regulatory processes, and conduct outreach on issues such as tariff changes.

USAID is guided by internal environmental regulations requiring an environmental review of all activities it implements. Those activities that might have a significant impact on the environment require a rigorous environmental impact assessment; environmental assessment best practices include the evaluation of potential social impacts as well as consultation of the affected community during the assessment process. Such activities must also respond to host country environmental regulations, which typically have similar assessment requirements. If a project receives funding from a multilateral development bank, it must also meet that institution's social and environmental review requirements. Many of the anticipated Power Africa activities will put USAID in the role of providing technical assistance and other support to ensure the successful completion of power generation or transmission projects that are implemented by another party, often private. In such cases, Power Africa will seek to ensure that the activity is informed by an environmental impact assessment that follows good EIA practices.

Importantly, USAID and other U.S. Government (USG) partners take specific measures to ensure that typically underrepresented members of the community—women and youth—have a voice in these processes. USAID implementing partners are required under their agreements with USAID to specifically assess and incorporate the impact of youth and gender in their technical assistance approach, emphasizing the importance of underrepresented elements of communities in the design, implementation, and outcomes of these efforts. More broadly within the Power Africa Working Group (comprised of 12 U.S. Government agencies), the interagency is exploring opportunities to build upon analysis that OPIC has conducted on implementing additional best practices for community engagement.

Much of our assistance requires community engagement far beyond consultation, especially when local partners and stakeholders play a direct role in project implementation or otherwise benefit from the assistance in question. For example, in Baringo County in Kenya, Power Africa is supporting an innovative biomass fuel project which allows local farmers to sell wood to a biomass plant which will then convert such materials into steam to produce electricity. The farmers' prior practice was to burn the wood into charcoal which they then sold at a lower price than the price they do now through the biomass plant. The biomass project will reduce environmental impact while increasing both power availability and economic opportunity for the farmers.

Community engagement and ownership is critical to ensuring the sustainability of Power Africa's investments. In Liberia, Power Africa is supporting the establishment of local community cooperatives to own and operate renewable energy microgrids. Through the U.S. African Development Fund Off Grid Challenge, implemented in partnership with General Electric, Power Africa awarded six $100,000 grants to support sustainable renewable power generation initiatives at the community level. The selected projects offer creative, community-driven solutions and highlight prioritized need. For example, Kenyan suppliers will expand delivery of pay-as-you-go lighting options to households in rural areas, while another awardee, TransAfrica Gas and Electric, will power cold storage facilities with solar systems for farmers and fishermen. A biodigester from another awardee, Afrisol Energy, will produce electricity for small businesses in Nairobi's urban settlements. The Off Grid Challenge has enabled a high level of innovation and community participation, and will be expanded to all six Power Africa countries later this year.

Question. World Bank President Jim Yong Kim has said, ''If we don't confront climate change, we won't end poverty.'' We understand that developing countries in Africa are relatively low—CO_2-emitting countries. We also understand that these countries need better access to electricity in order to become full partners in our global economy and to ensure effective delivery of social services, such as public health, education, and the like. This is going to require a delicate balance in our approach to Power Africa.

- ◆ How can we make sure that we reach the goal of providing electricity in underserved populations without compromising our climate change goals?
- ◆ What has the administration done to limit the possible negative environmental impact of Power Africa?
- ◆ The development of fossil fuels carries social and environmental costs over a range of areas: access to land, access to water, water pollution, air pollution and the resulting health impacts, and of course climate change. How have environmental and social assessments been incorporated into the choice of energy technology employed in the Power Africa Initiative's efforts?
- ◆ How does it help Africa leap-frog forward toward a truly sustainable and efficient renewable energy based economy? Please describe any clean energy projects supported by the Initiative.

Answer. Rural electrification rates are well below 5 percent in many areas of sub-Saharan Africa—the lowest in the world and significantly lower than average rates in Asia and Latin America. People who lack access to cleaner, more affordable energy spend significant amounts of their limited income and resources on costly and unhealthy forms of energy like indoor fires for cooking and expensive diesel to run factories. Without light, children can't study and businesses can't operate after dark. Without electricity, life-support machines and newborn incubators in hospitals don't function. Without refrigeration, food, and medicine go bad before ever reaching those who need it. Without modern cooking fuel, homes are filled with dangerous smoke and fumes. Better access to energy will multiply our investments in reaching the Millennium Development Goals by improving health, education, and household income.

Sub-Saharan Africa has tremendous untapped potential coming from renewable energy sources including through wind, solar, and geothermal. East Africa's Rift Valley has the potential to produce up to 15,000 MW of geothermal energy. Through Power Africa, the U.S. Government and its private sector partners are bringing technical expertise to accelerate the development of these resources.

Power Africa intends to reach the goal of providing electricity in underserved populations without compromising our climate change goals by engaging in power sector projects that use a sustainable mix of generation technologies, focusing on the use of renewable for off-grid and mini-grid solutions and helping Power Africa focus countries to build the necessary regulatory framework and institutional framework to encourage the use of and investment in renewable technologies so they can be scaled up from small levels of use. The Power Africa approach provides the opportunity to help the six focus countries use significantly cleaner generation technologies as well as utilize a greater level of renewable technologies. Power Africa is also providing critical institutional capacity building and assistance to develop the energy policy framework to manage the integration of renewable resources into several Power Africa countries' power gird on a more sustainable and reliable basis. A prime example of this is our work in Kenya helping the government and Kenya Power and Light manage the integration of wind and geothermal power into their grid while mitigating the risks to the stability of the grid because of the intermittent nature of the renewable resources.

Power Africa represents a new way of doing business for USAID. USAID's level of involvement in any particular transaction varies widely and may not involve directly developing, implementing, and/or funding any transaction-specific assistance. Under Power Africa, USAID seeks to partner with private sector entities that demonstrate concern for environmental sustainability and innovative approaches to incorporating these concerns into activities. Although USAID may not directly contribute to particular transactions such that USAID can dictate the scope of the activity, USAID selects priority transactions based in part upon the extent to which the project promotes the use of renewable technologies, as well as project viability (e.g., affordability, bankability, environmental, and social impact) and political and policy impacts and government support. Where USAID does directly engage in an activity facilitating infrastructure investments, USAID fully adheres to the Regulation 216 environmental compliance procedures.

By the time Power Africa is reviewing a project for engagement, the technology/energy source has already been selected by its private sector developer and investors. Although individual agencies may differ slightly in how they evaluate projects for assistance, Power Africa will review a project using the following criteria:

- Primary impact (MW, access, efficiency, reliability);
- Catalytic impact (potential for replication, larger projects);
- Private sector leadership and interest (global, local, U.S. partner);
- Clean energy resources;
- Project viability (affordability, bankability, environmental and social impact, etc.); and
- Political and policy impacts and government support.

When evaluating whether Power Africa will engage on a project, we prioritize cleaner and renewable energy sources and we review the relevant and available Environmental and Social Impact Assessments to understand whether the project is viable and sustainable.

Currently, Power Africa is supporting 26 transactions that are expected to reach financial closure by July 2014, with the potential to add over 5,000 MW of power in the six Power Africa countries. Power Africa leverages partnerships with the private sector and other donors and the incentive of private sector investment to accelerate the financial close and the construction of power generation projects to expand the availability and access to power. These 26 priority projects represent a variety of generation technologies and sizes.

In order to accomplish our goals for increased access under Power Africa, we are focused on expanding the distribution of power, enhancing the affordability of power and increasing access through mini-grid and off-grid projects. Given the constraints to expanding access through grid extension alone, the Power Africa Initiative is aligning new and existing small scale activities under more targeted framework: an initiative-wide strategy for mini-grid and off-grid power that will bring together the tools, expertise, and resources available from the 12 USG agencies working under

Power Africa. This strategy builds on existing efforts by multilateral agencies, USG initiatives, the private sector, NGOs, and other practitioners to address issues around energy access and to foster clean and renewable energy solutions in partnership with investors and NGO networks, particularly in rural areas.

The choice of a renewable technology does not automatically make mini-grid and off-grid projects sustainable. Power Africa focuses much of its effort in this space on ways in which we can scale up off-grid and mini-grid efforts that have been successful on a smaller scale and identifying business models that will make these efforts self-sustaining with local buy-in. With financial and technical support, the Power Africa strategy will seek to test and invest in different business and project models, identifying technically and financially sustainable solutions for small scale energy. The strategy will focus around two main components: Policy and Quality Assurance Framework and Finance.

In addition to the off-grid/mini-grid strategy, Power Africa supports a number of clean energy projects. Through the U.S.–Africa Clean Energy Financing Facility (ACEF) sponsored by the Overseas Private Investment Corporation (OPIC) and U.S. Trade and Development Agency (USTDA), Power Africa has provided grants for clean energy projects including a 5 MW solar plant in Tanzania as well as a $200,000 ACEF grant used for the software design and supply chain management for pay-as-you-go solar home systems in rural Tanzania. Specific examples of clean energy project supported by Power Africa include:

- USADF: Solar World (E.A.) Ltd. will construct five solar water points to provide water and electricity in a semiarid area of Kenya. TransAfrica Gas and Electric will power cold storage facilities with solar systems for farmers and fisherman in Nigeria.
- Corbetti Geothermal 1,000 MW, Ethiopia: Ethiopia's first private generation project was developed by Reykjavik Geothermal, a U.S. company, with the assistance of a Power Africa transaction advisor.
- Lake Turkana 300 MW Wind Project, Kenya: The Power Africa team provided technical advice that gave Lake Turkana's lenders comfort that the electrical grid could absorb the intermittent power associated with wind. The team also worked with the AfDB to secure needed financial guarantees.
- Kipeto 100 MW Wind Park, Kenya: Power Africa, through OPIC, is providing financing to Kipeto Energy, as well as providing technical advice to the Kenyan Government.
- NextGen 5 MW Solar Project, Tanzania: Power Africa, working with other donors, convinced the Tanzanian Government to increase the length of a standard PPA from 15 to 25 years so that NextGen, an American company, could access financing. The OPIC/USTDA U.S.-Africa Clean Energy Financing Facility (ACEF) provided a grant to support this project.

Question. What benchmarks and metrics are set out to guide and evaluate Power Africa? Is there a need to set some sort of cost-benefit ratio or criteria for authorizing Power Africa projects?

Answer. Power Africa has developed an interagency monitoring and evaluation (M&E) framework and plan that track progress toward the 10,000 MW and 20 million connections goals announced by President Obama in Cape Town, South Africa, in late June 2013. Through the interagency Power Africa Working Group (PAWG), we have established a M&E subworking group that has representatives from each of the Power Africa agencies. We've defined a set of 33 indicators that USAID and other members of the PAWG analyze and reports annually to benchmark and guide our efforts. These indicators range from tracking planned, closed, and commissioned transactions and their renewable energy mix to the reliability and distribution of power.

Benchmarks and indicators are based upon the overarching objective to increase access to reliable, affordable and cleaner energy. Specific benchmarks and indicators include measuring:

- The number of planned generation transactions in each of the six Power Africa focus countries;
- The number of MW's of generation capacity supported by the U.S. Government relating to the 10,000 MW and 20 million connection goals;
- Clean energy policies and the number of new laws passed or being implemented related to climate change;
- The national energy mix of each country; and
- The reliability of existing power resources including calculating the number of incidents and hours of power loss per month.

Initial results will be made public in August 2014 when Power Africa releases the Initiative's first annual report.

In addition, Ex-Import Bank tracks U.S. jobs created or sustained as a result of its financing (e.g., every 1 billion dollars in exports supported by Ex-Import Bank supports approximately 6,000 jobs).

We do not believe that there is a need to formally establish a cost-benefit ratio or criteria for authorizing Power Africa projects because Power Africa priority transactions/projects are being advanced by private sector developers and investors. These private sector partners would not advance these projects if they did not already meet some level of return and their cost-benefit analysis. Any mandated cost-benefit ratio or criteria remove a great deal of flexibility from the process, could create a significant burden for implementation, and would be duplicative of a process that is already being carried out by private sector partners.

GE Power & Water
Distributed Power

Biogas Distributed Power Solutions: Opportunities for Power Africa countries

GE Power & Water
Distributed Power

March 20, 2014

Biogas Distributed Power Solutions:
Opportunities for Power Africa countries

What is Distributed Power?

Today, more and more emerging countries are considering the use of distributed power technologies. Originally established when Thomas Edison built the first power plant in 1882, distributed power technologies are used to provide electrical and mechanical power at or near the point of use.

When deployed, distributed power technologies create a decentralized power system within which distributed generators meet local power demand through the network. This stands in contrast to central power plants, which provide energy to the entire power network via transmission lines from a single centralized location.

They can be used to provide continuous, intermittent, peak or even back-up power. Distributed power systems may be connected to the grid or off-grid. Some distributed power systems send excess electricity back into the grid; others are used exclusively for on-site energy needs.

The rise of distributed power is being driven by the same forces that are propelling the broader decentralization movement. These technologies are more widely available, smaller, more efficient and less costly today than they were just a decade ago.

Distributed power systems can be incrementally added to meet growing energy needs. Furthermore, distributed power systems in terms of fuel source are flexible, and are duel fuel capable. These systems also eliminate the need for expensive and capital intensive transmission projects because they are at or near the point of use; thus serving as a more realistic route for meeting critical energy needs.

In addition, some distributed power systems can leverage domestic natural resources and address environmental benefits. Countries are facing increasing pressure to utilize wastes and residues effectively and sustainably, while also deploying renewables. The use of biogas distributed energy systems allows governments to support renewable energy targets, leverage natural resources, while also providing much-need power to their citizens.

Biogas as an Energy Source

The disposal and treatment of biological waste presents an opportunity in many emerging countries as governments look to leverage natural resources, implement environmentally sound energy systems and address the growing need for power.

Anaerobic fermentation—a superior alternative to composting—provides a unique solution for the management of a wide range of organic substances. Created during anaerobic fermentation, biogas serves as a high-energy, renewable fuel that can be used as a substitute for fossil fuels. Biogas engines not only improve waste management, but also generate an economical energy supply.

Biogas results from anaerobic fermentation of organic materials. As a metabolic product of the participating methane bacteria, the prerequisites for its production are a lack of oxygen, a pH-value from 6.5 to 7.5 and a constant temperature of 60 to 80°F (psychrophile), 80 to 115°F (mesophile) or 115 to 130°F (thermophile). The fermentation period is approximately ten days for thermophiles, 25 to 30 days for mesophiles and 90 to 120 days for psychrophile bacteria. The fermentation systems of today operate largely within the mesophile temperature range.

The process of biogas generation is divided into three steps:

- Preparation of the bio-input
- Fermentation, and
- Post-treatment of the residual material

At the start, the organic material is collected in a primary pit, sterilized to remove harmful germs in case of food waste and moved to the digester. The biogas produced in the digester is collected in a gas storage tank to ensure a continuous supply of gas, independent of fluctuations in the gas production. Finally, the biogas is fed into a gas engine.

The end product from the fermentation of the biomass can be utilized as fertilizer. The gas mixture produced in the digester consists of 50 to 70% methane (CH_4) and 30 to 50% carbon dioxide (CO_2). This composition makes biogas well suited for combustion in gas engines.

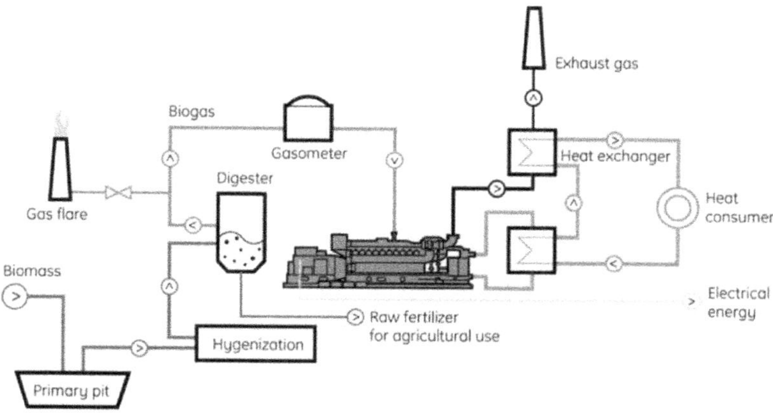

The generated electrical energy can be utilized for the treatment plant as well as to supply the public power grid. The thermal energy can be used for heating the digester or to offset the heat requirements of the treatment plant.

Additionally, compared to fossil fuels – utilizing biogas in the engines avoids any additional greenhouse gas emissions; due to the organic nature of the components of biogas, burning it in a gas engine for power generation emits the same amount of CO_2 into the atmosphere as was originally absorbed during the process of photosynthesis in the natural CO_2 cycle.

Furthermore, the remaining substrate from the digester can be used as high quality, agricultural fertilizer. This is done by neutralizing the acid effect with a higher ph-value. This process will keep nutrients retained and is nearly odorless.

Among others, the following organic materials are suitable for the generation of biogas. The figures in brackets show the biogas yield in scft per ton of moist material:

- Liquid manure, solid dung (700 – 2,500)
- Biomass from municipal solid waste (MSW) stream (3,500 – 4,200)
- Corn silage, non-food grains (6,400 – 10,500)
- Grease trap content (5,300 – 10,000)
- Used cooking fat (35,000)
- Grass, e.g., from EU set-aside areas (5,300 – 7,000)
- Biowastes from slaughter houses (3,500), breweries and distilleries (700), fruit and wine press houses (1,100), palm oil mill effluent, dairies (900), the cellulose industry or sugar production (1,400 – 2,100) Wood is not suitable for biogas production because the lignin it contains is indigestible to methane bacteria. Pesticides, disinfectants and antibiotics also have a negative effect on the bacteria and on biogas formation.

Opportunities in Tanzania and Ethiopia
There have been several initiatives throughout Africa to support biogas projects, including the Tanzania Domestic Biogas Programme and the Africa Biogas Partnership Program (ABPP). Established in 2008, the ABPP aims at constructing 100,000 biogas plants in Ethiopia, Kenya, Tanzania, Uganda, and Burkina Faso, with the goal of providing about half a million people access to a sustainable source of energy by the year 2017. We applaud these efforts; however, these programs are aimed primarily at residential, rural biogas projects.

To increase power supply to a larger universe of the population, Power Africa should consider fostering several large-scale biogas installations that will provide a roadmap for future development of biogas projects, with an initial focus in Tanzania and Ethiopia.

There are significant benefits as to why Power African should focus efforts in Tanzania and Ethiopia:

- The feedstock in Tanzania and Ethiopia is largely from agricultural based economies;
- Specifically in Tanzania, there exists a large sisal industry;
- Tanzania has an attractive diesel displacement tariff and also a mini-grid structure;
- Ethiopia is a major horticultural center, producing significant quantities of flowers for Europe; and
- Large greenhouse operations can provide more synergies, which includes providing feedstock, taking waste back as compost, and potential CO2 flooding of greenhouses

While we strongly encourage the development of biogas projects in sub-Saharan Africa, we also recognize the challenges tied to these projects, which include:

- Ethiopia has no feed in tariff structure in place;
- Off-takers can have liquidity challenges; and
- Most biogas projects require a significant investment in anaerobic digestion; companies that own the technology have not been keen to come to Africa

GE Solution
Jenbacher cogeneration technology enables customers to realize the maximum economic and ecological benefits available from utilizing biogas for power generation. More than 2,500 Jenbacher biogas systems with a total electrical output of over 1,900 MW have been delivered worldwide.

These plants generate about 15 million MW-hours of electricity a year – enough to supply more than 1.4 million US homes. Generating this amount of electrical power with biogas could average about 141 billion scft of natural gas a year. To operate a Jenbacher cogeneration plant with an electrical output of 500 kW, the dung of about 3,500 cows, 40,000 hogs or 1,500,000 laying hens is required.

Jenbacher biogas engines are certified as "ecomagination" products by GE. Only those technologies that provide a high level of both economic and environmental benefits are included in GE's ecomagination portfolio. Jenbacher engines are cost-effective and highly efficient so that they provide customers with high quality energy services while simultaneously reducing fuel use and environmental emissions.

Conclusion
With more than two-thirds of the population of sub-Saharan Africa without electricity, we applaud the efforts of Power Africa to add more than 10,000MW of clean, efficient energy in the six partner countries. Some may view the goal to double access to power in sub-Saharan Africa as daunting; however, this is an opportunity to build on Africa's enormous power potential and expand the reach of energy solutions throughout the region.

Distributed power systems are fast, diminishing the lead time required for first power and accelerating the compounding benefits of economic growth that is created by increased electricity availability. Biomass utilization in power generation can spur economic activity via the fuel collection process. Furthermore, electrifying rural areas via this process can slow the process of urbanization, and the costs and social issues it creates.

We would welcome the opportunity to discuss next steps with the Power Africa team. One option may be to conduct a biogas feasibility study focused on Ethiopia and Tanzania.

www.ingramcontent.com/pod-product-compliance
Lightning Source LLC
Chambersburg PA
CBHW080429290526
45791CB00008BA/2434
* 9 7 8 1 5 1 5 2 6 5 8 9 4 *